THE ANGELS

edited by

ROBERT SARDELLO

contributors

GAIL THOMAS   ROBERT SARDELLO
JOANNE STROUD   THOMAS MOORE
ROBERT D. ROMANYSHYN
PACO MITCHELL   DONALD COWAN
LARRY DOSSEY   FREDERICK TURNER
LOUISE COWAN   DONA S. GOWER
ROBERT TRAMMELL   EILEEN GREGORY
LYLE NOVINSKI   MARY VERNON
THERESE SCHROEDER-SHEKER

CONTINUUM • NEW YORK

1995

The Continuum Publishing Company
370 Lexington Avenue
New York, NY 10017

Printed in the United States of America

Library of Congress Cataloging-in-Publication Data

The angels / edited by Robert Sardello
   p. cm
   Originally published: Gathering of angels. Dallas : Dallas Institute
Publications, Dallas Institute of Humanities and Culture, © 1990.
   Includes bibliographical references.
   1. Angels—Congresses. 2. Angels in literature—Congresses. 3. Angels
in art—Congresses. I. Sardello, Robert.
[BL477. G28   1995]
291.2'15—dc20

                             95-32348
                                CIP

DEDICATED BY THE FELLOWS OF THE DALLAS INSTITUTE TO

DRS. LOUISE AND DONALD COWAN

in gratitude for their continuous and unfailing inspiration to those following the vocation of a life of thought. Like the angels, whose tasks in the cosmos are to guard the continuity of the great past in the present, cherish the quest and aspiration of the soul to create, protect by warning, informing, and helping, thereby defending the good that exists within each person, Louise and Donald Cowan are guardians and guides of these tasks in culture, the world of the heart, where the eternal resides within the provisional. From these two great teachers we have learned to seek truth, and in seeking truth to find the world as a work of divine creative art, and in finding the world in this way, to come unexpectedly upon joy.

CONTENTS

Angels and Science

Angels and Imagination

Angels and Art

Practical Work with the Angels

Editor's Preface

The Dallas Institute of Humanities and Culture has held two conferences on angels. The first, entitled "A Gathering of Angels," was held on February 24–26, 1989, and produced the papers first published under that title in 1990. The second conference, "Working With the Angels," was held on March 14, 1992, and was accompanied by an exhibition of angel paintings by Santa Fe artist Cynthia Smith Stibolt. Her *Angel of the Future,* originally in watercolor and gold, graces the cover of this book.

This new edition of *A Gathering of Angels,* retitled simply *The Angels,* includes three presentations from the second conference. First, Gail Thomas leads us, in a powerful way, to experience the angelic worlds in daily life. She recalls for us the intimate relation between nature spirits, or devas, and the angels. Further, she proposes that what we can most learn from the angels is how to grow our own wings through a deeper sense of desire and destiny. Therese Schroeder–Sheker brings the invaluable dimension of music and singing as a mode of relating characteristic of the angels. And, if music and rhythm belong to the angelic way of being, our most direct access to them is through singing. One does not have to be a trained musician, nor even versed in the tradition of sacred music. All that is necessary, says Therese, is a vivid presence to silence and holy solitude, which will issue in true singing from the heart. The third of the new presentations describes some meditative practices for becoming oriented toward the angels, something of the work we are required to do to establish an ongoing relation to the angels. We hope that these three additions, all of a practical nature, add significantly to this already rich collection.

The work of birthing this new edition into a real book was carried by Janis Lilly and Adrienne Cox. Their care and attentivness to each detail, in order to bring about something truly beautiful, is evident on each page that they have touched with the assistance of their angels.

Robert Sardello
Great Barrington
November 1994

INTRODUCTION

TO A GATHERING OF ANGELS

When we began to think about presenting a conference on angels at the Dallas Institute, the idea was whispered around quite softly at first. For here at the Institute, where really important issues such as public education, the teaching of teachers, and designing a master plan for the city of Dallas in the year 2000 occupy a good deal of time and effort and have a high profile, would there be any interest in something as intangible and seemingly impractical as angels? Well, around that time, the German film *Wings of Desire* was showing, and it aroused a good deal of discussion among the Fellows of the Institute. This interest made it possible to speak a little louder about getting together and talking about angels. None of the Fellows thought this strange or odd; to the contrary, everyone I talked to had a secret or not so secret interest in angels and was delighted about the prospect of an angel conference. In the ten years I have been putting together various programs, this one by far had the most enthusiastic reception. Something quite mysterious, I began to feel, was going on.

A sign of the times, perhaps. Ramtha, Lazaris, Kevin Ryerson, and many other channels have made contacting spiritual entities both popular and profitable. However, the willingness to pay attention to these channels indicates a growing cultural realization that we are in need of help. Furthermore, we might be ready to ask for help. And that readiness to ask for help connects us again to a much longer and deeper tradition which offers a different kind of help than channelling. An angel never interferes with nor takes over one's consciousness, or in any way counters the freedom of the human. Thus, angels are far more subtle than, if I may say, the denser entities who are the source of channelling.

Rather than introduce these papers by saying why we should give attention to angels, I want to indicate what will occur if we do not learn how to establish relationships with the angels. On October 9, 1918, Rudolf Steiner presented a lecture in Zurich called "The Work of the Angels in Man's Astral Body." Steiner, as you may know, was the originator of Anthroposophy, the study of the wisdom of the human spirit. He says in this lecture that the present age—up until around the third millennium, that is up until about the year 2000—is given the task of consciously becoming awake and aware of the angels. During this time, the angels are seeking to come into connection with our conscious, waking lives. The angels are inclined toward us, but we must consciously, freely, be inclined toward them. They have a work to do for humanity; this work will take place regardless, says Steiner. However, if we are not consciously and freely working to establish a relationship with them, angel work will show up as symptom and pathology.

In Zurich, home of C. G. Jung, Steiner repeats for the spirit what Jung had stated for the soul. Jung says that in the symptoms of the soul are the gods. Steiner says that in the symptoms of the spirit are the angels. What symptoms in particular? First, Steiner indicates, and not out of speculation but out of a conscious clairvoyance, there will occur in culture a prevalence of certain kinds of sexual difficulties. Remember, this is Steiner talking in 1918. His exact words are:

> Certain instinctive knowledge that will arise in human nature, instinctive knowledge connected with the mystery of birth and conception, with sexual life as a whole, threatens to become baleful if the danger of which I have spoken takes effect [i.e., if we do not become consciously aware of the angels]. Certain angels would then themselves undergo a change—a change of which I cannot speak, because this is a subject belonging to the higher secrets of initiation—science which may not yet be disclosed. But this much can certainly be said: The effect in the evolution of humanity would be that certain instincts connected with the sexual life would arise in a pernicious form

instead of wholesomely, in clear waking consciousness. These instincts would not be mere aberrations but would pass over into and configure the social life, would above all prevent men—through what would then enter their blood as the effect of the sexual life—from unfolding brotherhood in any form whatever on the earth, and would rather induce them to rebel against it. (p.26)

What could he be talking about? That is something to let the imagination work on.

Then, Steiner goes on to speak of a second symptom. Everything connected with medicine, he says, will make a great advance in the materialistic sense. We will acquire knowledge of certain substances and certain treatments—and thereby do terrible harm. But the harm will be called useful. The harm will be called health–giving.

And then, Steiner speaks of a third symptom. Man will get to know of definite forces, which, by means of certain manipulations, will enable him to unleash tremendous mechanical forces into the world—and the whole of technical science will sail into desolate waters. But, he says, human egoism will find these desolate waters of tremendous use and benefit.

We need only to reflect for a moment on the very large difficulties culture now faces within the three areas of sexuality, medicine, and technology to know that Steiner saw in 1918 the possibility of our refusal of the angels.

I introduce these concerns here, at the start of these papers, to indicate something all of the essayists feel: the concern for angels at this particular time is serious business. We live in a time of great change, a period in which it is possible to make preparations for the forming of a new culture. This culture will either be dominated by fear and the task of survival or recognize spiritual reality actually present in the world as active force. If the latter is chosen, new capacities of perception, knowing, and action need to be developed, capacities enabling everyone to participate in the subtle dimensions of reality. The following essays contribute to the development of that larger sense of reality and point toward the creation of a spiritual culture that does not abandon the material world.

Perhaps I can assist your reading of the papers by offering an Ariadne's thread to hold on to as you go through the labyrinthine worlds of psychology, science, literature, and art in search of the angels. What most characterizes the following, I believe, is the attempt to work out of the present circumstances of consciousness so as to seek break–through points indicating the presence of the angels. That is to say, none of these writings works within esoteric traditions nor asks or requires the reader to be an "initiate." Rather, all of the contributors begin with the world as we now know it, with ordinary consciousness, and seek the mystery which lies right in front of us. The careful reader will find, here and there, statements concerning the kinds of disciplines needed to begin feeling the nearness of angels—the importance of silence and stillness, emptying out, giving attention to words and language, appreciating rhythm as a world phenomenon, healthy terror, the capacity of "almost seeing." But nowhere will be found a doctrine or a set of established practices to follow because the aim does not consist of taking up a religious or spiritual practice other than the practice of daily approaching the temple of the world in a spiritual manner.

One of the intricate passages in the labyrinth leading to the angels concerns the role of science. On the one hand, a number of the authors show that the angels withdrew or were banished from the world with the development of natural science as a mode of consciousness. Robert Romanyshyn, in particular, has pursued this development in a most astute manner, showing how science reduces multiple planes of reality to a single, material plane. On the other hand, those very same papers that point out the difficulties of science also look to science as now crossing the threshold and finding again the spiritual worlds. I believe it is necessary to distinguish the prevalent materialism of science from the historical and cultural development of consciousness which is signaled by the onset of science. As a mode of materialism, the angels will never be rediscovered through the procedures or findings of physics, biology, or astronomy; one must be a little bit aware of the possibility that the angels are being reduced to natural phenomena. However, science as an indication that the human spirit is in the process of development from a kind of dream-like state which existed from pre–history up until about the fifteenth century, characterized by the capacity to have direct perception of the spiritual worlds, to the point where an objective view of the world excludes spiritual presences, shows the task now necessary. When spiritual presences accompanied a dreamlike perception of the world, there was no choice involved on the part of humanity concerning participation with spiritual beings. Nice, but naive commingling. Scientific consciousness, taken as a development of the human spirit, brings loss of spiritual worlds but also makes possible the choice to seek connection with clear and fully awake consciousness. Thus, in some of the papers you will find some rather astounding recent scientific findings. However, it is not the findings in themselves that are the breakthrough but, it seems to me, the choice to look upon these phenomena in a truly spiritual manner.

An additional aspect of this collection is the felt importance of tradition. None of the authors, it seems, cares much for "new age" language. I am afraid my own contribution comes dangerously close to that, and I am grateful to be surrounded by those steeped in the sense of tradition. Tradition simply recognizes that the work lies in adhering to the wisdom of the ages, of re–creating this wisdom in forms suitable for present times. Tradition does not imply rigid repetition of the past; it does require a real feeling for the past as not past but continuing into the present and shaping the future. Not the least aspect of this sense of tradition involves never forgetting the world. As Gail Thomas so beautifully develops it, if we forget the seasons, we forget the angels. Seasonal consciousness, too, belongs to tradition. Then, also, there is plenty of room within tradition for differences. For example, Larry Dossey adheres quite strongly to the tradition of angelic hierarchies, while Donald Cowan makes room for equality; both views are within tradition.

The contributions in this volume also present wonderful contradictions which assure that you are not being told what or how to think about angels but to go and find out for yourselves. An extraordinary feature of a community such as the Fellows of the Institute is that major differences in each others' work are appreciated. Thus, in one paper, that of Fred Turner, a view that angels will perhaps be created through genetic engineering is juxtaposed with Louise Cowan's view of an absolute division between the realm of the angels and the realm of the human, a view she supports with her reading of Dante. These contradictions spark the imagination and prevent "angelology" from being confined to one sector of the world, thus thwarting a kind of consciousness eager to judge one side as evil and the other as good.

Finally, I wish to point out one more dimension of this work on angels, and that is the force of the angels. You will find very little sweet talk here about the angels and instead a wonderful absence of sentimentalism. Plenty of mystery, yes. But at the same time, most clearly presented in Robert Trammell's paper, real strength and healthy terror are instilled, which makes clear that adequate preparation of the vessel of the soul is required to face the angels. As Dona Gower wisely warns, there is a tendency in the tradition of angels toward disembodiment and abstraction. That kind of angelic imagination will not be found in these papers; indeed, it is even suggested by Eileen Gregory, in her skillful reading of the poet H.D., that terrible events such as war, rather than a retribution for cultural wrongdoing, is an apocalyptic uncovering of the angels.

You can perhaps begin to see why we felt that it would be of service to have the presentations of this conference on angels made available in published form. There are a number of works around that give accounts of the history of angels and of the classical classification of angels. There are some "new age" publications which present sweet views of the angels and how to contact them for personal help. And there are esoteric approaches to angels that approach them from the magical traditions. But a cultural view of angels—that, to my knowledge, has not been available until now. Making such an approach available, we hope, constitutes a service to the angels.

ROBERT SARDELLO
Dallas 1990

ANGELS AND THE SOUL

ANNUNCIATION

THOMAS MOORE

During the years I lived in a monastery I awoke each morning at roughly 5:00 A.M. to the words *"Ave Maria."* I would struggle into consciousness and answer this greeting from one of my confreres with *"Gratia Plena."* This was a small ritual intended to keep in mind the sacred order of the day and to recall the theological focus of the order—the Virgin Mary.

Ave Maria. During all those years, without thinking of it, I was speaking in the dialect of angels. In particular they are the words of Gabriel, the Archangel, spoken at the moment of one of the most important turning points in the Christian mystery, "annunciation." Traditional translations of this dialogue between Mary and the Angel are close to the original Greek, and they are familiar to anyone brought up in Christianity. But I would like to present a fresh translation in order to bring out certain nuances. The passage is from the Gospel of Luke:

> In the sixth month Gabriel, the Angel, was sent by God to a Galilean city called Nazareth, to a virgin who was engaged to a man named Joseph, of the House of David. The name of the virgin was Mariam.
>
> Coming into her presence the angel spoke: "Hello, favored one. The Lord is with you. Among women you have been blessed."
>
> She saw him but was troubled by what he said. She wondered what kind of greeting this was. The angel said to her: "Don't be afraid, for you have been graced by God, and indeed you will conceive in your womb and give birth to a son, and you will give him the name Jesus. . . ."

But Mariam said to the angel: "How can this be since I am not intimate with a man?" In response the angel said to her: "The Holy Spirit will approach you, and the power of the highest will cast a shadow on you, and the Holy Thing which is born will be called the Son of God. . . ."

Mariam said: "Listen! The Lord's servant! What you have said, let it happen to me." And the angel left her.

Like the epiphanies James Joyce celebrated in his stories, ordinary moments full of significance and insight, annunciations happen every day in the plainest of circumstances. Religious festivals like the Annunciation always call to mind eternal happenings, forms and images that give structure and value to every life. The Angel and the Virgin are always engaging in dialogue: the angel announcing some impossibility, the virgin taken aback, questioning, agreeing. In this particular event the soul—virginal, patient, expectant, prepared, receptive, modest—begins to carry new life and personality, a child, as the paintings often show, miraculously fully formed from conception. (Every time we use the word "concept," an annunciation, probably hidden and forgotten, lies in its history.) Jung says of the Child archetype that the infant thing appears "smaller than small, bigger than big."[1] Significantly the Gospel calls the infant a holy thing, as though recognizing that what is divinely born can be anything. Paintings portray the child as simultaneously an infant and aging.

Now let us look closely at some of the particulars of this prototypical annunciation. The angel greeted Mary. *Ave*—hello. This little word, "*ave*," is an important one. The angel is known by his greeting. According to the text, Mary is troubled not only by what the angel says but also by his greeting. An angel's greeting is indeed a shock. It is like a friendly word from a sphere entirely remote and other. A few nights ago I was awakened from sleep when I heard my name being called from the next room. It was the middle of the night, and I was alone in the house—I thought. Over the years friends have told of seeing winged figures in their homes, and they have met up with people who seem to be playing a role more in their soul's story than in ordinary life.

According to tradition angels often take human form. Fifteen years ago I was on a bus traveling through the night between Amherst, Massachusetts and Syracuse, New York. Toward the beginning of the trip a group of people boarded, including a young woman who sat a couple of seats behind me. I had just completed an intense weekend of meditation and spiritual exercises. After a while the young woman moved up to the empty seat next to me. "Hello," she said. (You see what I'm getting at.) She then told me many things about myself. I felt comfortably but strangely transparent. It seemed as though I were in a field of magic, and the laws of nature had been interrupted. I had a strong desire to hear more and talk and get to know this woman as a person, but just then the bus arrived in the small town of Lenox, and she walked to the front and stepped down into the darkness. My office is located now just over the hill from that bus stop, and when people ask, as they so often do, how I happen to be living in that remote part of western Massachusetts, having moved from Texas and having never lived in New England, I immediately think of this night angel.

The "*ave*" is important. Angelic "separated substances," to use Aquinas's technical description of angels, fill every inch of world and every person and every event. Origen said, "Everything is filled with angels." Still, since they are, again in the abstract language of classical theology, created but not material, it is easy to overlook the angels and miss their *aves*. Still, their hellos are signals of grace. Sixth–century medallions depicted the scene of Annunciation on one side, while the word "*kaire*," the Greek form of *ave*, was imprinted on the other. These medals, it is said, were used for white magic, as amulets of good health.

Tradition praises Mary as a model for dealing with angels, for her readiness to acknowledge the angel's greeting, and of course for her willingness to embrace the fate announced by the angel. Paintings show her in a contemplative mood, in her room, reading. It would seem to take a degree of expectancy and intellectual preparedness to glimpse the angel when he appears. Without that Marian attitude, that yoga of the anima, the angel passes unnoticed. And if the angel passes, nothing is announced, nothing incarnated. Life may feel symptomatically empty.

St. Bernard of Clairvaux, in his commentaries on Annunciation, focuses attention on Mary's humility. "The soul that is humble," he says, "even if she has to lament the loss of her virginity, may nevertheless be pleasing to God."[2] Humility is easily sentimentalized and turned into self-denigration. But humility is an important virtue of psychological life that allows things to happen, allows a world to exist beyond the one we know and understand. It is one of the most important psychological attitudes, required if we are to return to a life graced by angels. In her humility Mary shows genuine respect for the angel. But think of our modern approaches to angelic hellos. We find it difficult to offer respect to any greeting from the world to us. Taking all subjectivity and therefore "greeting" to ourselves, we cannot listen when we are addressed. Yet psychological life begins in these greetings addressed to us. People often report dreams in which some person or animal or thing wants the attention, if not the love, of the dreamer but has to go by, neglected or feared. This slighting of the figures who greet us, more than family history or trauma, plays a role in psychological confusion, depression, obsession, and the rest. With no commerce between the human and the angelic, there can be no connection to the ground of one's life. The angel, as Wallace Stevens says in *Angels Surrounded by Paysans*, is necessary.

In this world without angels that we call modern, the very idea of an event or action implies something happening according to the expectations and modes of the day. The word "modern" means "measured by the day." But the work of angels is of a different order. According to an old Irish story, an angel in the form of a bird (dream animals may be angels in disguise), more beautiful than all the birds of the world, sang three tunes to St. Mochaoi. It seemed to the saint that he was listening to this heavenly music for a full hour, but in fact each melody lasted fifty years. When he returned to his monastery, no one knew him, and an oratory had been erected in his honor. Another Irish saint, St. Brendan, informs us that bird-angels sing music while they are perched on the branches of the Tree of Life. An angelic sensibility does not reason by the modes of the day but rather according to eternal dimensions. Angel time is not human time. Just this factor alone would transform our way of looking at our lives and our society. To break out of the modern time zone of diachronous life would be to discover the mediation of the angel and to move closer to the mythic groundings of life. The angel announces and effects the soul's fate in relation to eternal issues that only brush against the situations of life.

Because angels by definition do not fit into the modern world, we find it difficult to give them the respect they require. For instance, we are quick to label visitations from these other circles "hallucination." The word is from the Greek *alein*, related to our word "aleatoric," meaning chance, as in the toss of dice. We think annunciations are random, chance, irrelevant events. They do not seem to have the weight and importance of caused and situated happenings. Again, we fail to see intention and plot unless it comes from us. But this is an ego–centered point of view. It would be better, instead of reducing angels to hallucination, to consider hallucinations under the rubric of angelology.

This comment leads me to a slight digression on theology. What I like about a conference on angels held at an institute of humanities is the doing of theology outside the classrooms of an academic religion department. Theology belongs to us all, whatever our denomination or practice. If it has any value, theology is deeply quotidian. It does not have to be reduced to the interpretation of a particular church or text. The concerns of theology are immanent, in the world, in us, in daily life, in society. I don't see how we can survive if we ignore theological issues, thinking that society can get along with the social and natural sciences. How are we to find our way through rituals, images, beliefs, ethics, mysteries, marriage, possessions of the soul, and so on, if we have no accessible theology? In fact, we don't get away with it. We find ourselves in a disturbing split, with fundamentalism, moralism, and ritualism on one side, and pure secularism on the other. There couldn't be plainer indications that we suffer the loss of the mediating angel than daily news reports of this secularism and fundamentalism gone mad.

When theology is rooted in a spiritual viewpoint, it turns to philosophy in quest of meaning and orderly presentation. Its practice is done in the church and tends either to become cut off from the flow of daily life or to develop doctrinal and moral conclusions that are then applied to life. From the perspective of soul, theology might recognize that every day a person makes gestures, confesses, sacrifices, expresses contrition, communes with the world and with friends, eats symbolically, hypostasizes alcohol or some other drug, decides morality, and lives on what he believes. Religion is deeply quotidian, and its study, theology, could reflect that context.

When psychology is narrowly defined, however subtly, against a medical background and then is allowed to take up themes of human life that do not belong to it, such as substance abuse, hallucination, marital discord, and so on, it immediately reduces these issues, brimming with theological implications, to humanistic, secularistic failings of Promethean society. Mysteries become problems. Problems are there to be solved. Theology, in fact, goes underground and unconscious. It appears as the salvational fantasy with psychology, unthinkingly assumed and rarely questioned.

But theology need not always be salvational. As Ivan Illich has been arguing of late, we do not need psychotherapy to save us from human suffering. We can define theology with the same degree of depth James Hillman has given psychology. Theology, etymologically, is the logos of the divine. Thinking theologically we search out the divine nature, what I have been loosely calling—following Tillich—the grounding of life, in everyday issues. Theology is the perception of the sacred, especially in those areas of life wrongly supposed to be secular. Theology articulates the holy and the taboo, the angel and the devil, sacrament and fetish, virtue and vice, and the eternal words that speak of the soul and not only of life. Jung was aware of the profound richness of the Western theological tradition as a resource for today, but he chose to turn all of that subtle theology toward his psychological system. In Jung the deep blue tones of theology change to the reds and yellows of psychology. An alternative approach is a transparent conception of theology itself that does not rely on the social sciences, or even upon depth psychology, for relevance, language, or interpretation.

In the story of annunciation the role of virginity obviously is crucial. The soul is virginal as it waits to receive the greeting of the angel. Waiting itself, so carefully depicted in the paintings of annunciation, is the work of the virgin soul. Rather than short–term therapy we might take more interest in long–term waiting. As Ficino says, when the external act decreases, the internal act is strengthened. Religions generally instruct us in formal manners of waiting, as in Lent and Advent. It is a time for fewer activities and less food, for more meditation and postures of expectancy. If psychotherapeutic practice had the angel in mind, it might become concerned with technologies of waiting, preparing for the angel's greeting.

The Marian soul is virginal but not naïve. This virgin is educated. Notice in paintings of annunciation the refinement of architecture and dress. Mary is usually sitting before an open book, her fingers on the pages. She is the virgin *sophia*, the sophisticated virgin. Meister Eckhart offers some insight into this virginity when he says: "Virgin designates a human being who is devoid of all foreign images, and who is as void as he was when he was not yet."[3] He goes on to explain that he does not mean a lack of intelligence. He is describing a person who is not attached to certain images or a definite body of knowledge.

I take this to mean that when our minds are closed on strict interpretations of our lives and our world, we are not disposed to angelic orders. The angel announces things that contradict what we know to be true. In the moment of annunciation the soul becomes pregnant miraculously, without human intercourse. This pregnancy has nothing to do with products of reason or experience or understanding or trial and error. Our educational systems, based on these modern methods, are not set up for angelic revelations. The virginal attitude requires an emptying out—kenosis, the old spiritual teachers called it. Dreams often show episodes when the soul is voided: precious things are lost or stolen, or there are extravagant scenes of toilets and eliminations. This kenosis, following Eckhart, is preparation for annunciation.

The obvious defense against kenosis is to rush to fill any voids that are felt as emptiness, longing, need, hunger, thirst, or deprivation. The virginal soul is not easy to find or maintain. This is part of the more general difficulty of giving anima or soul a place. But artful waiting has its rewards, even if the waiting is archetypal, eternal, never satisfied. I do not want to suggest that waiting is prelude to fulfillment. In a strange way, the angel's announcement is the conception. Waiting and fulfillment are one act. The virgin, the angel, and the dove are all present at once. Waiting is announcement is conception.

Paintings of annunciation also portray a refined but palpable sexuality. The question of angels and eros is a difficult one. We often link angels with innocence, children, and figures whose wings are much more prominent than their private parts. However, it seems to me that sexuality is deeply involved in angelic encounters. In the Infancy Gospel of Pseudo–Matthew, a gospel story from the ninth century, Joseph returns from a job away from home to find Mary pregnant. Her virgin companions say to him: "We know ourselves that no man has touched her; we know ourselves that, in her, innocence and virginity were preserved unspoiled. For she has been guarded by God; she always persists with us in prayer. Daily an angel of the Lord speaks with her; daily she accepts food from the hand of an angel. How is it possible there should be any sin in her? If you want us to voice our suspicion to you, this pregnancy was caused by none other than God's angel."

I am not suggesting that the angel made love to Mary. But from a certain point of view annunciation is nothing but divine intercourse arranged through the angel go–between. Mary is impregnated—perhaps, as Augustine says, through the ear. Paintings show a golden stream flowing straight from the Holy Spirit to her. Is this spiritual semen? Is annunciation a scene of subtle sex, as of the subtle body?

In annunciation the soul is spiritually cast in shadow. Wouldn't anyone admit that at crucial moments in life one's reasoning, plans, understanding, and self–image are all obscured by an unexpected and uncalled–for darkness? Bernard offers some thoughts on the notion of "overshadowing" which emphasize the confusion a new movement of soul can bring. "The manner in which you will conceive by the Holy

Spirit will be so veiled and covered and overshadowed in his most secret counsel by Christ . . . that no one will have knowledge of it except him and you. . . . It can't be learned how except by her in whom it shall be accomplished."[4] The pregnancy of soul granted by annunciation cannot be explained. It would be good if we gave up the attempt. It can only be known in the intimate contact between the spirit and the virgin soul. In the act itself is the revelation of meaning. In any form of soul–work it might be better to give up rationalization and do what the painters do— trace the scene, amplify the setting and the dialogue, and participate poetically in annunciation.

Scenes of annunciation also hint at a theme of considerable interest in modern linguistic analysis: the sexual nature of language. The soul becomes pregnant through what is heard. Words impregnate. In many paintings the angel points to a banner on which his words are printed, thus emphasizing the word, written and spoken. The importance of words for angels comes through in the reflections of Anne Catherine Emmerich, a nun who was a visionary and stigmatic. She lived from 1774 to 1824 and had visions concerning the life of the Virgin Mary. In her description of annunciation she says: "It was the Angel Gabriel. He gently moved his arm away from his body as he spoke to her. I saw the words issuing from his mouth like shining letters; I read them and I heard them."[5]

Bernard also emphasizes the importance of words: "For God, word is the same as deed. For God alone it is the same thing to do as to say."[6] In annunciation word is efficacious. But the word has to be heard and read. We have to "read" the message of the angel. In general, reading in this sense seems to have gone out of style. Instead we interpret, analyze, or apply our understanding of a thing toward an improved life. Rarely do we "read" the Bible, "read" our dreams, "read" experience. Therapy is a kind of reading and is perhaps one of the few places where the angel's words are taken seriously. But therapy exists in a world that doesn't know how to read the everyday. Everything has an angel's banner that can be read, if it is only seen and valued. If the paintings are correct, then the primary work of angels is to point. They point to what is to be read. Experience, we could say, is not meaningful as much as it is expressive. It has its own logos. Its word is its presentation of itself. The world expresses itself and wants to be heard, seen, and read. The angel, bringer and pointer of words, is the go–between of reader and what is read.

Reflection on angels and words, however, requires that we realign our notion of language. Consider the following statement of Igor Stravinsky talking about his musical setting of *Oedipus Rex*: "What a joy it is to compose music to a language of convention, almost of ritual. The very nature of which imposes a lofty dignity! One no longer feels dominated by the phrase, the literal meaning of the words.... [The composer can] concentrate all his attention on its primary constituent element, that is to say, on the syllable."[7] This is the language of the angel—non–discursive utterance; not meaningful sentences, but beautiful, resonant, musical, allusive, imagistic, polyvalent syllables. The break–up of language enslaved to the expression of its human author is the liberation of language to do its primary job, impregnation of the soul through the ear. Language greets us, calls for a relationship, breaks in upon us a world that is unfamiliar and fateful. And this incursive utterance of the world is the gist of annunciation.

Stravinsky's interest in syllabic expression leads us to see all language as mantra. Listening to the ritual nature of language, its syllabic history, its syllabic allusions, nourishes the soul rather than the spirit of language. We hear the words, as if they were being pointed out syllable by syllable, rather than the abstracted meaning of the words. Experience, too, can be appreciated as syllabic. As Anne Catherine Emmerich says, she both heard the words and read them. It is not enough to interpret and understand. We also have to hear the sensate presentation of experience in its expressive pieces, not only in its aggregates of meaning.

Dreams syllabize life by taking its components out of the sentences by which we find meaning and exploding them into new, rich suggestiveness precisely in their syllabification. When experience is uttered and read piece by piece, as in Stravinsky's music of the Oedipus story, the poetic mind emerges. This poetic mind, the gift of the angel, is radically different from the discursive mind. Its words signal secret, unknowing impregnation. Discursive language, that is, any expression taken for its intention and meaning, is not carried out in the presence of virginal consciousness, and it is not angelic, not sexual, not fruitful. "Blessed is the fruit of your womb," the angel says to Mary.

Annunciation takes place in a closed space the natural medium of which is not air or any of the usual elements. Philo of Alexandria says that angels belong properly in the quintessence, in the ether, the medium of the universal soul or *anima mundi*. If we are to read our lives with the guidance of the angel, we have to be lifted, sublimated in a certain sense, out of the crass elements into quintessential fantasy. Origen says that angels like to read the sacred Scriptures. Mary is shown reading the Scriptures as the angel appears. But this is not reading in the usual sense; it is quintessential reading.

Finally, angelic expression moves from radical poetry to music. Hundreds of paintings show angels playing a variety of instruments. Perhaps the purest poetry is the music of the soul, its rhythms, pitches, harmonies, discords, its tubas and guitars, psalteries and rebecs. We find them all in the hands of angels. We might recall, as we think of medieval and early Renaissance paintings of angels as musicians, that universities of the time defined music as a quality of the world and of the soul. Musical sounds were only imitations of this quintessential music.

The angel draws attention not only to the syllabic poetry of the expressive world and life, but also to the music. The ultimate music therapy is an appreciation for the musical forms and timbres life enjoys. If we think we should always play the same tune or sound in the same timbre or always be in sonata or dirge or gavotte, then we do not recognize the angel musician who always reveals divine intentions to the human ear.

In order to spell this out further, I would like to cite a rather long and wandering, but pregnant, passage from Proust's *Swann in Love*:

He knew that the very memory of the piano falsified still further the perspective in which he saw the elements of music, that the field open to the musician is not a miserable stave of seven notes but an immeasurable keyboard (still almost entirely unknown) on which, and there only, separated by the thick darkness of its unexplored tracts, some few among the millions of keys of tenderness, of passion, of courage, of serenity, which compose it, each one different from all the rest as one universe differs from another, have been discovered by a few great artists who do us the service, when they awaken in us the emotion corresponding to the theme they have discovered, of showing us what richness, what variety lies hidden, unknown to us, in that vast, unfathomed and forbidding night of our soul which we take to be an impenetrable void.

Annunciations are happening all the time, manifesting the infinite variety of the soul. Without a virginal accessibility to angels, however, we sense the soul as a void. We call it "the Unconscious," a negative name which implies that the world we know has more variety and substance and consciousness than that other realm where angels soar and make music. Could it be that our social problems with drugs indicate a cultural attempt to open to that angelic order? In the Greece of Aristophanes, when poetic sensibility was lost, ambassadors were sent to the underworld to try to return the old poets. Perhaps some of the underworld events of our society are the embodiment of that desperate journey. But another way is to return to the conviction held passionately by extremely intelligent theologians in our history that everything has its angel who keeps us safe from unholy life. The angels, says Origen, "always behold the face of the Father who is in heaven and see the divinity of him who created us."

The angel is the go–between, keeping human life in touch with its divine and mysterious ground. In *The Steps of Humility* Bernard says, "Some of the Seraphim check your impudent and imprudent curiosity that you might not be allowed to pierce the mysteries of either heaven or of the Church on earth" (X. 35). The angel also protects the mystery. Gabriel does not offer explanations. He only tells Mary what is happening at the moment, and he gives a few hints about the future. Even as he reveals, he conceals. The angel's wing preserves mystery. Symptomatically we long to find ways to oblivion and ignorance. This is an honorable intention and represents a deep need of the soul. In a positive sense, religion is the opiate of the people. To sink into mystery, to say *"fiat"* to imponderable fate, is to feed the soul on the bread of angels.

Wings that conceal even as they bring messages suggest the need to find language and to go about the work of theology in a way that does not flatten and over–expose the mysteries. This sensitivity to sacred secrets was a preoccupation of medieval and Renaissance theologians, such as Pico della Mirandola, who planned to write a book on this theme entitled *Poetic Theology*. Maybe it is about time that book was written. It was based on the idea that mysteries can only be apprehended through initiation, not by discursiveness. Annunciation is a great mystery. In his book *Convivium*, Ficino advised always being prepared for the angel. But how do we prepare except as Mary did, through prayer, meditation, and an imagination open to the angelic?

It goes against modern sensibility to preserve rather than expose mystery. But that tendency makes it all the clearer how much work needs to be done toward a new poetic theology. One way would be an iconographic method that understands poetic and imagistic presentations of theology as more significant than the reasoned approaches. It used to be said that European cathedrals were Bibles in stone, a way illiterate people could be exposed to religious teaching. But one can imagine quite the opposite. A brilliant leaded window, a roof–perched animal, a doorway saint, scene upon scene from the Bible and history, figures of great persons—this architectural iconography is a method for keeping eternity in the minds of us all, even the most sophisticated, syllable by syllable. Bernard advised keeping the door to one's room closed in order to keep out the world, knowing, however, that angels can pass through doors.

Reason and explanation, taken literally rather than for their imagination, are impenetrable to angels. Aquinas's book on separate substances could be read as a collection of syllables.

Another clue to the angel is to be found in Pico's poetic theology. He made extensive studies in Christian theology, Jewish mystical writings, and Greek mysteries. His friend and teacher, Ficino, wrote his own long volume on Platonic theology and also relied on many religions for his insights. Ficino laid out a five–fold hierarchy: God, Angel, Soul, Quality, Body.[8] For him the angel is timeless, without place, but composite, that is, comprising in himself the root fantasies of all created things. For Ficino the angel holds and disperses the multiplicity of life. To encounter Ficino's angel is to meet the pure light of the divine radiating into the multiplicity of worldly life. We are back at annunciation and incarnation.

The theological issue of incarnation in daily life turns into earthly questions: Should I marry this person? Should I take that job? Should I move east or west? Incarnating the fantasies fate has seeded is the mystery that provides the deepest existential anxiety and yet offers the only hope of a blessed life. This is the sexual mystery of annunciation. How can my soul conceive and bear fruit? The only way is by preparing for the angel, to be willing to be "overshadowed," to be able to say, "What I hear being said by things and events, let it be, *fiat*. I do not understand it at all. I may never know what it is all about. I hope my husband and my family can tolerate me having been intimately touched by a bird–spirit in the presence of and through the negotiating of an angel. I have no idea what I'm setting myself up for, but I do know that the only way to fulfill my virginity, my absolute possibility, that fertile feeling of void that is shaped from not knowing what I am doing here, is to acquiesce to the angel who is privy to the very grounding myths of my identity."

This meditative, intelligent humility, brimming with holy imagination, is the ultimate cure for the masochistic symptoms that bring so much suffering. We could do no better than mime the Virgin who sits in her room, a hand on the pages of the Scriptures, poised to receive the angel and to read his banner.

So Fierce Its Streaming Beauty,
So Terrible Its Averted Gaze
On Once Encountering an Angel

Robert D. Romanyshyn

It was the stillness that was most impressive, a kind of stillness that I had felt only once before, in Africa, the stillness of the early morning of the world, before we came. It was not that I was aware of the silence. Rather it was only that there was the silence, a silence wrapped within itself, complete, fulfilled, without need for sound. This silence was its own consciousness, aware of itself as a slow, rhythmic, vaporous liquidity, the mist of the early morning of the world, floating, condensing, dissolving, congealing in a sleepy kind of dumbness. And the light, yellowish white, spreading itself with the mist, textured, itself a palpable thing, diaphanous, the veil of the world's first morning, gathering itself, and in the next moment an appearance. Formed, out of nothing but this light, a being so composed within itself, so tranquil, unstirred by the mist, calm, serene, beatific. A being so beautiful, before distinctions, neither male nor female in form nor young nor old in face, neither conscious nor unconscious, neither aware nor asleep. Creation's first image, before time, eternal, unmoved, so peaceful in its splendid indifference. Creation itself, the whole of it. So fierce its streaming beauty, so terrible its averted gaze. The mirror of our failure, the measure of our loss.

I shall not tell you the occasion of this encounter, the second of three, except to say that the occasion, the setting, mattered, and to add that some work which I was doing at the time, and about which I will speak in a moment, seems in retrospect a kind of preparation. But I have begun in this way because it is the truest thing I can say about the Angel, and the best. Against its silence all else that I have to say seems a rather feeble effort to evoke that moment, to keep it open. I had wondered and thought about the Angel before this encounter, but now I wait for its appearance and watch for its signs. The words, then, serve that function, the work of keeping a place, of continued preparation.

Who is the Angel? The struggle with this question became for the poet Rilke the *Duino Elegies*. He says:

> Every Angel is terrible. Still, though, alas!
> I invoke you, almost deadly birds of the soul,
> knowing what you are. Oh, where are the days of Tobias,
> When one of the shining–most stood on the simple threshold,
> a little disguised for the journey, no longer appalling,
> (a youth to the youth as he curiously peered outside).
> Let the archangel perilous now, from behind the stars,
> step but a step down hitherwards: high up–beating,
> our heart would out–beat us. Who are you?
>
> Early successes, creation's pampered darlings,
> ranges, summits, dawn–red ridges
> of all beginning,—pollen of blossoming god head,
> hinges of light, corridors, stairways, thrones,
> spaces of being, shields of felicity, tumults
> of stormily–rapturous feeling, and suddenly, separate,
> mirrors, drawing up their own
> outstreamed beauty into their faces again.[1]

Imaginal beings? That seems too poor. Symbols then? That is no better. Certainly, however, the poet does persuade us of the immense gap between them and us. Witnesses, then, who by their presence bear witness to the higher degree of the reality of the invisible, to what, perhaps at the right moment, can be experienced only out of the corner of one's prepared eye. Hence, too, they are so *terrible* to us who still depend upon the visible.

Inspiration, too, and humiliation; consolation perhaps, if the mood is right, but always terror. Simultaneously, the being who validates our highest but dimmest aspirations and who reminds us of the distance between what we are and would become. Or perhaps it is equally true to say, of what we are and what we (once) were? Certainly, however, the Angel is not us, and if in any way in relation to us, then as frame which bounds us, by displaying what we are *not*: the *Other* which the human imagination veers toward but never reaches, the shapers of our sense of the real.

An unbearable reality, this Angel. A heavy burden, a yoke of sadness, an impossibility. Rilke, meditating on angel *and* beast, gives us our place:

> And yet, within the wakefully–warm beast
> there lies the weight and care of a great sadness.
> For that which often overwhelms us clings
> to him as well,—a kind of memory
> that what we're pressing after now was once
> nearer and truer and attached to us
> with infinite tenderness. Here all is distance,
> there it was breath. Compared with that first home
> the second seems ambiguous and draughty.
> Oh bliss of *tiny* creatures that *remain*
> for ever in the womb that brought them forth!
> Joy of the gnat, that can still leap *within*,
> even on its wedding–day: for womb is all.
>
> . . . .
>
> And we, spectators always, everywhere,
> looking at, never out of, everything!
> It fills us. We arrange it. It decays.
> We re–arrange it, and decay ourselves.
>
> Who's turned us round like this, so that we always,
> do what we may, retain the attitude
> of someone who is departing? Just as he,
> on the last hill, that shows him all his valley
> for the last time, will turn and stop and linger,
> we live our lives, for ever taking leave.[2]

Between the beast and the angel, between the sleepy dumbness of the one and the perfect narcissism of the other, we are suspended, always at a loss, forever taking our leave. But we also have been left, and in the distance between us and creation there is the quest—the quest to make ready and to welcome the presence of the absent Angel. In the distance, between the silence of one and the other, there comes the human voice.

> Who, if I cried, would hear me among the angelic
> orders? And even if one of them suddenly
> pressed me against his heart, I should fade in the strength
>   of his
> stronger existence. For Beauty's nothing
> but beginning of Terror we're still just able to bear,
> and why we adore it so is because it serenely
> disdains to destroy us. Each single angel is terrible.
> And so I keep down my heart, and swallow the call–note
> of depth–dark sobbing. Alas, who is there
> we can make use of? Not angels, not men;
> and already the knowing brutes are aware
> that we don't feel very securely at home
> within our interpreted world. There remains, perhaps,
> some tree on a slope, to be looked at day after day,
> there remains for us yesterday's walk and the cupboard
>   love loyalty
> of a habit that liked us and stayed and never gave notice.
> Oh, and there's Night, there's Night, when wind full of
>   cosmic space
> feeds on our faces: for whom would she not remain,
> longed for, mild disenchantress, painfully there
> for the lonely heart to achieve? Is she lighter for lovers?[3]

Tom Moore speaks about the "Ave" of the Angel, about the Angel and annunciation, about the task of the Angel being to guard the virginal aspect of the soul awaiting an annunciation.[4] But Rilke asks, "Who if *I* cried . . . ?" The Angel was "Ave" and we were addressed. Now we call, in anguish as Rilke knows, for its return. Have we grown deaf? Deaf to the silences? Even the animal knows, according to Rilke, that we are not really at home within our interpreted world, within the world *we* have spoken. Where is the Angel? How have we made ourselves inhospitable to *its* call?

The work I was doing when the encounter with the Angel occurred was a study of the cultural–historical origins of linear perspective vision in fifteenth–century Italian art. The invention of this way of seeing, as if you are staring, one–eyed, through a window at a world receding toward a vanishing point, or as if you have a camera eye on the world, has become a cultural convention, a habit of mind, a disposition of the soul. Through its development and under its influence we have become spectators of a world, which has become primarily a spectacle, a matter of light, inhabiting a body which has become primarily a specimen. Of the many values which this vision has inscribed upon the soul of modernity, not the least of which is the hegemony of vision or the rule of "the despotic eye," the one which surprisingly and unexpectedly touched upon the angel was the transformation in depth which this vision achieved.[5] According to Alberti, who in 1435 codified the steps required to give the appearance of three–dimensional depth on a two–dimensional plane, that is to make a painting appear as if it were a window on the world, linear perspective vision creates a space in which the viewer and all beings or objects viewed lie on the same plane. In short, linear perspective vision is the condition for ex–plaining the world, for making the world a matter of ex–planation,

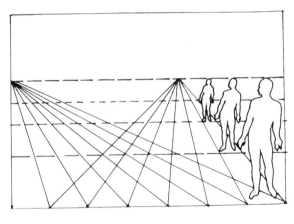

Figure 1

for reducing (leveling) all levels of existence to the same plane. Depth as a matter of horizon–tal spatial distance between the seer and the seen began to eclipse depth as a matter of vertical levels.[6] The illustration depicted in Figure 1 summarizes these points. In that homogenous space of linear vision all objects shrink from the bottom up toward the head as they recede toward the horizon line, and the objects, which all lie on the same horizontal plane, remain below that horizon line.

The world explained, the world within which all levels of existence are reduced to the same plane, is inhospitable to beings who belong to other levels. In the mapped, geometrical space of linear vision, beings, like angels, who do inhabit another depth or level of reality progressively lose their place. The window through which the detached spectator observes the world, a window which Alberti called a veil and which was actually a grid, projects an objective landscape of evenly spaced grid coordinates, and from that space beings, like angels, are destined to be banished and to become mere mental phenomena, mere subjective realities. Figure 2 illustrates this projective vision thrust upon the world. It depicts how this way of seeing actually is destined to become an unquestioned model for what is seen. Through the gridded screen the artist-see–er not only sees the world, he also envisions it in that specific fashion which pretends an equality, a homogeneity amongst things. By placing the Angel within the same space of humanity, linear perspective vision makes

Figure 2

humanity the equal of the Angel. If that consequence was unintended, its effects have been nonetheless catastrophic for Angels and for us.

A very brief history of the Angel in painting would easily confirm the fact that the chief effect of this vision which reduces the Angel to our level has been the disappearance of the Angel. Simone Martini's *Annunciation*, which dates from 1333, vividly displays the majesty of the Angel, as does Sassetta's *Mystical Marriage of St. Francis* which dates from 1437. These two paintings along with da Vinci's *Annunciation* of 1472, illustrated in Figure 3, clearly show that the Angel who enters the human world inhabits it in a different way and belongs to another dimension or depth of reality. With the increasing success of linear perspective vision, however, the Angel's majesty is progressively eclipsed. While the Angel lingers, a supporting structure, like clouds, will be introduced to ground the Angel in our world. Eventually, however, even that lingering presence will prove too much, and the Angel will be further removed by being humanized as it is, for example, in Rubens' *Garden of Love* dating from 1632. Here the Angel as Eros has become Cupid, and little, if any, of its majestic difference remains. Perhaps a final humiliation of the Angel within the space of linear vision is Joseph Vien's *The Merchant of Love*

Figure 3

Figure 4

from 1763, illustrated in Figure 4. Here the Angel is not only subject to the measure of science by being placed within that space where it is an object to be ex–plained, it is also subject to the measure of economics by being placed within that space where it is an object for sale. Between Martini's Angel and Vien's we have erased the Angel. Or perhaps it is closer to the truth of the Angel to say that between these two epiphanies, which lie on either side of that way of seeing which has created our modern world, the Angel has withdrawn. Perhaps the absence of the Angel is a sign of our defective vision, a vision which, in imposing its map of ex–planation upon the world, has become inhospitable to the world's mysterious depths.

    I want to conclude these words of preparation by telling a story of an event recounted in a California newspaper in January, 1987. At an annual meeting of the American Astronomical Association, astronomers reported the discovery of the largest bodies ever observed in the universe—gigantic luminous blue arcs nearly two million trillion miles long. Smooth and symmetrical in shape, these bodies of light could be mere accidents of observation, or a new class of space objects requiring a change in our current systems of explanation. Could it also be the case, however, that these giant luminous bodies are the way in which the Angel is breaking–through the neutral, homogenized, ex–plained, and de–sacralized world of our creation, restoring a sense of the awe–ful, *transcendent–depths* of the real? Could it be the case that these bodies of light are the Angel *breaking–through* at the margins, at the *breakdowns* of our systems of ex–planation, at the epitome of that very way of thinking, the physics of cosmic energy levels, of light, which initially invited the Angel to withdraw?

I do not wish to suggest here that the possible angelic reality of these luminous arcs is a matter only or even primarily of experimental investigation. Rather, realization of any of these three possibilities is primarily a matter of *attitude*. If the Angel's disappearance has had something to do with our defective vision, then perhaps its re–appearance also requires an adjustment in us. In taking the measure of the world, linear perspective vision has imposed its ways of speaking upon reality. It has projected its vision of the world as a language of ex–planation to be mapped upon the world. Perhaps the shift in attitude requires a speaking which arises out of listening, a saying which is primarily a re–saying, a speaking which is responsive to and response–able (able to respond) for the world. There are biblical accounts which tell us that the appearance of the Angel strikes one dumb, and I think that the encounter with the Angel which opened these words was a request for and an invitation to *silence*. Perhaps before anything else the Angel as "Ave," as annunciation, is an invitation to listen. I think here of those wonderful medieval paintings which depict the Angel's voice as impregnating the virgin's ear. If we follow this iconography as harbinger of the shift in attitude we are seeking, then the speaking which arises out of listening, out of *obedience* to the *audible,* is a pregnant speaking, a speaking already bearing the word of the other. My intention here has been to speak in this fashion, to speak as much as possible words that arose from that encounter with the Angel, and as little as possible words imposed upon that encounter. The intention was to make speech faithful to the silence out of which the Angel appeared.

RAPHAEL: GOD'S MEDICINE TO MAN

GAIL THOMAS

Let us consider the difference between the angelic and human life. In Sanskrit there is a word which covers the beings not of human form which belong to another dimension. The word is Deva, which means "shining one" or "being of luminous light." Deva includes an awesome diversity, from the most glorious archangel who reigns over the cosmos to the tiniest fairy living in the bud of the periwinkle.[1]

British teacher and writer William Bloom distinguishes the two realms. He suggests there is what might be called the atomic, of which the human is a part, and the devic, of which the angel is a part. The atomic—so called because of the particles and electric charges in constant movement which create physical shapes—consists of rocks, minerals, plants, animals, and humans; the devic realm includes sylphs, undines, salamanders, gnomes, elves, fairies, goblins, angels, archangels, cherubim, and seraphim.

Bloom argues that these two planes of existence work together to create what we call form or body. Devic essence "knows" and at all levels provides the pattern by which atomic matter can manifest into form. Devic life does the knowing and bridging while atomic life does the creative doing.

These two parallel life streams, working together, give us the shape, color, sound, smell, and feel of things as we know them. Yet, their orientation is in opposition to each other.

> The atomic or human is oriented to *doing*.
> The devic or angelic is oriented to *being*.

The atomic or human sees color and hears sound.
The devic or angelic sees sound and hears color.

The atomic seeks expansion.
The devic seeks focus.

The atomic is becoming aware of unfoldment.
The devic is becoming focused on creation.

The core form of the devic essence is that of a double spiral or double vortex. Above the double vortex is its focus of consciousness which is attuned to cosmic awareness. Extending downward and outward is an energy cape which may enfold the life with which the deva is working, a flowering plant or bush, for example. This cape acts as a guiding matrix within which that life might manifest.

This is also the role that I imagine an angel's wings to have. The wings, like a cape, enfold the person or entity, creating an opportunity for emergence into the fullest of being. For a person so wrapped, an archangel, Raphael for example, would be as close as breathing!

Raphael as breathing. What can be more immediate than breath? What closer image could we have to depict the angel of man, the one in charge of man's constant healing and the healing of the earth? What could be more intimate? As the angel of man, what could bring Raphael more immediately into our presence than through breath?

About ten years ago, when I was quietly and agonizingly writing poems of my own, one of them began, "And who if I cried would hear ME from the order of Angels?" Rilke's poem has been close to me for many years and I have read carefully, with surprising interest, the suffering he endured in writing the *Duino Elegies*. I have continued to be drawn to this poem, using phrases from it in writings, applying them, in many cases, to the work of the Institute on the city. It was not until we decided to have a conference on angels that I have come to understand my affinity with Rilke's great work.

Not knowing where to enter this conversation on angels, I put out the call to the universe for help, and the answer came early one morning during my meditation. Suddenly, the beginning of the "First Elegy" broke into the silence:

> And who if I cried would hear me from the order of Angels?
> And even if one suddenly held me to his heart: I would dissolve there from his stronger presence.[2]

And much to my surprise, I heard, quite audibly, the answer: "Raphael!"

I am confident that most of you know that Raphael is one of the archangels. Beyond that, you may be as much in the dark as I was. I knew that Raphael kept company with Michael and Gabriel and that he dined with Milton's Adam and Eve in *Paradise Lost* and told them the story of the Creation. I could remember from my childhood the story of Raphael and the healing fish, but nothing more. What I had not realized but was soon to learn is that Raphael is the angel of healing! His name means "God has healed."

Who is Raphael? According to the Zohar, "Raphael is charged to heal the earth, and through him . . . the earth furnishes an abode for man, whom he also heals."[3]

I am intrigued by this angel of healing. Suddenly, I sense this angel everywhere. I spoke last year (at a conference on AIDS) of an inner healer within each of us—a communication within the body, mind, and spirit that knows what is needed and asks for help from sources which remain constantly available within each person. Is this inner healer guided and informed by Raphael? Is this inner healer a microcosm of a healing essence within the universe which also is Raphael? These questions lead to a larger issue, an issue concerning the nature of healing itself. What is going on in the process we call "healing"? A close review of what is known about the image of Raphael may help our understanding.

Raphael first appears in the Book of Tobit, a book of the Apocrypha. He is a companion to Tobit's son Tobias on a journey. Disguising himself as a fellow tribesman, the angel accompanies Tobias on a difficult mission, teaching him to heal himself and others with the very thing that threatens him. At the end of the trip, Raphael identifies himself by name as "one of the seven holy angels that attend the throne of God."

I was surprised by the number seven for the archangels because in the Bible there are only three named—although I had run across this number in Robert Fludd's work.

The Hermetic philosopher Robert Fludd classifies seven planetary archangels, including Raphael, listing them in the following way:

Saturn	Zephkiel, the contemplation of God
Jupiter	Zadkiel, the righteousness of God
Mars	Samael, the severity of God
Sun	Michael, like unto God
Venus	Hanael, the grace of God
Moon	Gabriel, the strength of God
Mercury	Raphael, the medicine of God[4]

To see Raphael as Mercury helps in our understanding of the nature of healing. And it is not only Fludd who makes this connection; Milton compares Raphael to Mercury by referring to the angel as "Maia's son" who is the Greek Hermes. Rudolf Steiner also sees Raphael as Mercury. He says in his book, *The Four Seasons and the Archangels*, ". . . through the power of Raphael [man] can be led to perceive and recognize the healing principle, the great world–therapy, which lives in the Christ–principle." And later:

> All that can be learnt in this way under the influence of the great teacher Raphael—who is really Mercury in Christian terminology and in Christian usage should carry the staff of Mercury—can be worthily crowned only insofar as it is received into the mysteries and ritual of Easter.[5]

Rudolf Steiner sees the four seasons—summer, autumn, winter and spring—as the elemental expressions of the four archangels—Uriel, Michael, Gabriel, and Raphael. By suggesting a relationship between Raphael and Mercury and the Christian ritual of Easter, Steiner asks us to see more deeply into the Spring rite. He sees it as world–therapy, as a healing principle.

Using the four seasons as a medicine circle, or "genre wheel," Steiner imagines the four archangels as the forces in the seasons of the year. Gabriel as the angel of Christmas offers nourishment to the Earth's surface and inhabitants from salt crystals which have formed in the core of the inner earth during the cold and dormant winter. Raphael receives this nourishment during the Easter season and infuses it into man, animal, and plant life through the process of breathing. The forces that prevail during breathing heal us continually. They become spiritual forces in the summer, under the aegis of Uriel, as the healing elements rise to the head and become thought. Michael, guiding the season of autumn, forges with his mighty sword the thought forces into forces of will.

Raphael, as the essence of Easter, of death and resurrection and imaged by Steiner as breathing, offers an archetypal picture of the healing principle—the constant in and out of our breath—taking the outside in; as above, so below; as it is in the cosmos, so it is within each of us. It is also the pattern of finding and losing and the mercurial ways of Hermes. Raphael is connected with this realm of the constant flow of healing forces within and without humankind, crossing boundaries, finding, losing, winning, gaining. Raphael's charge is to heal the earth, and then mankind. The seasons are the Earth, breathing. Raphael's name means "God has healed"! Our experience of this healing is as a finding and losing.

Breath—the most intimate of human activities . . . Raphael is that close!

Let us look again at the Book of Tobit and the story of the angel Raphael. It is a story of losing and finding.

We are told that Tobit, a righteous man who has kept the ways of the Lord, loses his sight and is blind for four years. He sends his son Tobias to Media to collect the ten talents of silver he had left with a friend twenty years before. Tobias asks his Father, "How will I know the roads to take for this journey to Media?" Raphael appears outside the house, disguised as a fellow countryman, to act as guide to Tobias although the boy does not know he is an angel of God. Tobias' mother is grieving. She says, "Why must you send my child away? Is he not the staff of our hands, with his errands to and fro for us? Surely money is not the only thing that matters? Surely it is not as precious as our child?" Tobit answers, "Do not think such thoughts. Going away and coming back, all will be well with our child . . . . A good angel will go with him. He will have a good journey and come back to us well and happy." And she dried her tears.

Going away and coming back, a good angel will go with him; he will have a good journey. Is this not the story of healing, a losing and finding? A losing in order to complete a finding; sacrifice followed by sudden gain?

The first night on the road, the two are camped beside the Tigris river. The boy goes down to wash his feet when a great fish leaps from the water and almost swallows his foot. The angel instructs the boy not only to catch the fish but to cut it open and take out the gall, the heart, and the liver and to save them. Raphael uses the fish to heal the lives of Tobit, Tobias, and their kinswoman, Sarah. Sarah has been betrothed to seven husbands, but all have died on the wedding night, before consummation, killed by a jealous demon who has attached himself to Sarah. Raphael arranges for the marriage between Tobias and Sarah and teaches Tobias to cook the heart and liver of the fish in order to "smoke out" the demon. The text says: "The demon fled to Egypt. Raphael pursued him there and bound and shackled him at once."

After collecting the talents of silver and being given half the estate of Sarah's father, including servants, oxen and sheep, donkeys and camels, clothes, money, and household things, the entourage returns to Nineveh and the house of Tobit. Upon seeing his father, Tobias, as instructed by Raphael, places the gall of the fish upon Tobit's blind eyes, and his sight is restored:

Tobias came on towards him (he had the fish's gall in his hand). He blew into his eyes and said, steadying him, "Take courage, father!" With this he applied the medicine, left it there a while, then with both hands peeled away a filmy skin from the corners of his eyes. Then his father fell on his neck and wept. He exclaimed, "I can see, my son, the light of my eyes!" And he said:

"Blessed be God!
Blessed be his great name!
Blessed be all his holy angels!
Blessed be his great name for evermore!
For he had scourged me
And now has had pity on me
And I see my son Tobias."

The story of Tobit and his son Tobias is a tender one. It is no wonder we learned it as children. It talks to the child in each of us of the companionship of angels. It assures us that we are not alone, that there is a companion traveling with us who is a healing force in everything we do and are. The story tells us that our healing comes from our own adversity if we face it squarely. It also encourages us to risk and venture forth and not to be afraid of losing, failing, or sacrificing. The child in us begins to learn that it is in releasing that we find, in losing that we win.

It is in adult life that we suffer the estrangement of rational thought and the loneliness that comes from disbelief.

Certainly, Rilke's agony was a struggle to assume the childlike intimacy only his angel would bring. In the "First Elegy," he says:

Every angel brings terror.
So I withhold myself and keep back the lure of my
    dark sobbing.

And later:

Do you still not understand? Fling the emptiness out from
   Your arms
into the spaces we breathe: maybe the birds will
feel the thinner air with a more inward flight.

And Rilke knew his angel was Raphael. Listen to the beginning of the "Second Elegy":

Every Angel brings terror. And yet, woe is me,

My song calls upon you, near deadly birds of the
soul, knowing who you are. Where have the days of
Tobias gone when one supremely shining stood in a simple
doorway, disguised a little for the journey and no longer
   frightening;

(young to the young one as he curiously peered out.)

Should the archangel, the perilous one, behind the stars
   take a single step downward
and toward us, our own surging hearts would slay us.
   Who are you?

Well, I think we know. The one who is close, as breath itself!

Angels and the Spiral of Creation

Robert Sardello

From the fifteenth century to the present, a world–view recognizing the living relation between human beings and spiritual beings has gradually diminished to the extent that the bond of mutual development has been severely damaged. I am thinking, in particular, about the effect of this damaged relationship on the household of the earth. A devastating disturbance in the ecology of the whole results from looking outward and seeing the earth as a non–living backdrop of material processes for human use and consumption. Even with science and technology of a type that is careful and caring, an outlook of moderated materialism, the path of destruction is inevitable because the circulation between the spiritual and the earthly has been severed. And thus, earth is forced to function as a closed system, a circle without an opening, breaking the first law of spiritual wisdom. The ancient Egyptian Emerald Tablet (Hermes Trismegistus) states the law thus: "Combine the heavenly with the earthly in accordance with the laws of nature, and health and happiness shall be yours as long as you live."

Nature, says this law, is not a closed circle but an open spiral, with earthly beings and spiritual beings involved in each other's activities— always. Furthermore, the law indicates that the human task consists of learning to imitate this action.

This, then, is what I want to address. First, how are the angels present in nature, and second, what does the act of imitating the action of angels entail? To focus these questions, I shall concentrate on the so–called inanimate world of nature, rather than on the plant, animal, or human levels.

Each of us has had to contemplate the question, who are the angels? I see them as the creating presences within all things and all things as evidence of their presence. It is not, I believe, that all things are left on the doorstep of the earth by the angels without a trace of their source. Angels are messengers who are also the message; they are the things of the world in their activity. Seen through spirit, all things are angel activities, and for that reason, the material world makes a spiritual difference.

As a case in point of the heavenly within nature, the remedies which belong to that approach to healing known as homeopathy rely upon correspondences which exist between the pattern of planetary movements and this pattern as it is repeated in condensed form in the flowers of certain plants. If one traces the pattern of the planet Venus over a period of eight years, a picture presents itself that looks exactly like the pattern at the center of a silver thistle blossom. Homeopathic remedies are made from this flower for Venusian ailments such as genital infections. Thus certain patterns of movement in the extra–terrestrial, starry universe are found reflected in the microcosmic plant world; we see the same laws at work, although the periodicity differs. These kinds of patterns, quite inexplicable in terms of physical processes alone, I suggest are the visible traces of angels. The work of the angels takes place in the invisible; however, traces of angels always carry the mark of an authentic symbol, a uniting of what is above with what is below. Symbolic vision is thus required to see angel work, a mode of vision which is one level above imagination. Imagination is more passive than symbolic vision and consists of receiving an image which may remain incomprehensible for a long time. In symbolic vision, there is a flow active between the spirit and the imagination. If one looks at the planet Venus and then at a silver thistle blossom, that is, if one looks only with the senses, no relation can be seen. If one looks through imagination, a similarity between the rhythm of the planetary orbit and the pattern of the blossom becomes apparent. Look through symbolic imagination and you see an activity that is the same in both places, forming both planetary orbit and thistle blossom; this activity is angel work. Angels are the messengers, the go–betweens; it is their signature that makes the similarity between Venus and silver thistle, that makes the silver thistle a heavenly body here on earth.

The human task of imitating the ongoing, active, symbolizing relation between the heavenly and the earthly that is the mark of the angels in nature has been known for centuries within the disciplines of spiritual and psychic wisdom. As nature imitates the heavenly, so must man learn to do so consciously. The first discipline to be learned to achieve this capacity of working in harmony with the angels is meditation. The first arcana of the Tarot depicts this task, the work of the Magician. The Magician must learn to concentrate without effort. In the Marseille deck of the Tarot, which originated in about the twelfth century, the Magician wears a marvelous lemniscate hat, a hat in the shape of a figure–eight resting on its side. The hat images the balance of the two states of consciousness required for meditation/concentration, or the state of being fully awake, and complete relaxation, or the state of being asleep. The meditative state is man's conscious imitation of the unity of rhythm of the movement of the earth in its course between day and night, the balance between day and night. It is truly astounding how man, from earliest times, knew that if one looked with care at the material world, one would find there also the spiritual world; and by imitating the actions of the material world, the archetypal, spiritual, and psychic world opened to experience. Thus, we see first the presence of the angels in the vast cosmos working within the things of the world. Next we see that by paying close attention to the activities of the things of the world, the kind of consciousness necessary to bring the presence of the angels forward is disclosed. The angels are ever present but will not make themselves known unless the right questions are asked.

The angels that have the specific task of bridging the heavenly with the physical, material world are, in tradition, called the Thrones. In a cycle of lectures on the book of Genesis, Rudolf Steiner, a clairvoyant, presents a detailed description of these angels of matter. He says:

> Actually, when we penetrate through external matter, through
> the elementary covering of the earth, to what has made this

earth covering solid, it would be natural to feel the deepest reverence for the Beings we call the Thrones (spirits of will), who have labored so long in this earth element to build up the solid ground upon which we tread, and which we ourselves bear within us in the earthly constituents of our physical bodies. (p.77)

The Thrones belong to the triad that forms the first and highest hierarchy of angels. This triad consists of the Thrones, the Cherubim, and the Seraphim. The name Seraphim, understood in the sense of ancient Hebrew esotericism, is always interpreted as referring to beings who receive the ideas and aims of the cosmic system from God. The Cherubim, who belong to the next hierarchy, have the task of elaborating in wisdom the aims and ideas received. The Cherubim are thus spirits of wisdom, capable of transposing into workable plans what is indicated by the Seraphim. The Thrones have the task, figuratively speaking, of putting into practice the cosmic thoughts which have been conceived in wisdom, thoughts received by the Seraphim from God and pondered over by the Cherubim.

Now, we are used to images of angels as beautiful, winged, golden–haired, human–like beings. Thrones, Cherubim, and Seraphim are not in this image. In Ezekiel, the Thrones are pictured as many–colored wheel–like structures. These structures are built up in such a way as to form wheels within wheels, multi–colored transparent rings, one turning within the other, the inner one with eyes; and, it is said, they rise. Furthermore, it is said that the Spirit of the Cherubim resides in the rings that are the Thrones. A most complex, strange, incomprehensible picture of angels.

Thrones is a Greek word, meaning something like a chair, a seat. The essential thing about a throne or a chair is that it sustains, manifesting that faithful reliability which we can be so grateful for in "inanimate" things. When one feels this world as spiritual and does not relegate spiritual things to some other plane, it becomes possible to feel how the mineral world, for example, is actually the highest spiritual world. The "new age" interest in crystals has something to it, although the practices associated with it are most often directed toward self–gain rather than to connecting with the angels. In what sense might the mineral world be the highest of spiritual presences in this world? Quite simply, rocks are desireless within themselves. The human world is filled with tumultuous and conflicting desires. The animal world also has desire, known as instinct. And even the plant world has a kind of instinct about it, a life–force. But the mineral world is desireless, and as such is the perfect reflection of the Creator's desire. Hence, the Revelations of John speak of the heavenly Throne, the heavenly seat, in an image of the mineral world— "And He who sat there appeared like jasper and carnelian, and round the throne was a rainbow that looked like an emerald."

Thrones—the angels creating matter, the material world the trace of their presence, and their presence visible through the vision of symbolic imagination. As we try to approach these angels through thought, they are quite beyond us. Their strange appearance does not provide the possibility of identifying with them as do the more classical images of angels, for nothing about them reminds us of the human. How are these angels matter–creating? For an intimation of what they might look like, consider for a moment the phenomenon of UFO's, unidentified flying objects. The Dutch angelologist H. C. Moolenburgh, in his work *A Handbook of Angels,* connects UFO's with angels. So does Billy Graham in his book on angels. And both authors relate the UFO phenomena specifically to the higher hierarchies of angels.

Ten percent of the population has seen a UFO, so perhaps a good number of people have experienced the Thrones. Instead of imagining UFO's as material objects in space and time, we might do well to go more in the direction of Jung in his work on UFO's, understanding them as images of the soul of the world. I would say they are the beings who ensoul matter, who create living matter. Thrones appear at the threshold of space and time. I would imagine that is why UFO's seem to move in ways no physical object could possibly move—at infinite speed, changing direction without slowing down, appearing and disappearing.

What about the image in Ezekiel—the wheel within the wheel structure? If you have ever seen photographs of UFO's, you'd find them surprisingly similar to this structure. But do not be fooled into thinking that if they show up in photographs they are physical structures; rather they seem to me to be structures which create physical matter. Thus it comes as no surprise that there is so much argument about whether these photographs depict a "real" object or only some sort of natural phenomenon of light, of cloud formations, or of electrical energy. A UFO picture is always indeterminate but has nonetheless the wheel within a wheel form. Consider this analogy to see what may be presenting itself. When you are fully occupied with a thought, at the moment when there is nothing else present but the thought, at that moment, you are the thought—it is your identity. This is like the inner wheel. Now, when you let go of that thought, it does not disappear completely. You can recall it again at any time. The thought has become exteriorized. You and the thought are not fully identified as one any more; it is exterior now to the act of thinking—it is a manifested thought. The Thrones act in a similar manner, the inner wheel being the concentrated contemplation, the outer wheel being the manifest thought. The Thrones are, in effect, envisioning the material world, seeing everything in an interior way and also manifesting that interior thought as matter–creating. Furthermore, according to the description of Ezekiel, the wheels within wheels with inner eyes rise, a significant detail which speaks of the relation between the inner and outer wheel. It is this aspect of the image that prevents a purely mechanical interpretation of the movement of the UFO. If you follow this picture in your imagination, you will see that a wheel turning within a wheel may give mechanical motion, but not the appearance of something rising. The relation of inner to outer wheel—imaged not mechanically but spiritually, imaged through symbolic imagination—pictures a spiral, not two independent circles. A spiraling wheel within a wheel does not move in space but creates space.

When we contemplate the UFO image through symbolic imagination rather than through the senses—which would see a physical object that inexplicably does not obey the laws of physical objects—or an imagination which sees a spaceship full of extra–terrestrials, we might see the activity of the Thrones. One of the characteristics of angels is that they visit, that is, they appear now and then in the physical. A UFO is not a physical object, but something making an appearance in the physical, at the threshold. The pictures of these "craft" show quite clearly that they are not physical, but more the forming of a cloud–like substance with a rounded peak in the center of an inner wheel. Perhaps you feel reluctant to accept pictures of UFO's as Thrones, though I have tried to stay close to the image. However, I would much rather say that UFO's are presences of Thrones than that Ezekiel saw a flying saucer. I believe that all the talk of extra–terrestrials and spaceships is actually talk about angels in the metaphors of materialism—a denial of the presence of angels even when brought face to face with them. Furthermore, so–called UFO's behave in ways which are in keeping with the image of matter–creating beings. These activities include electromagnetic interference phenomena and witnesses being burned, experiencing intense heat, numbness, temporary blindness, and unconsciousness. Ignition systems of automobiles quit in the presence of Thrones, and when they disappear auto engines immediately restart, headlights burn again and full function is restored. Thrones are very powerful beings. We would not expect that they would bring in a piece of already solidified matter and set it down peacefully on earth. Reality, so to speak, would more likely have to step aside, make way for the continuance of creation.

Now, I know I may be coming very close to the limits of your willingness to suspend disbelief. But let us take one final step. What might imitating the activity of the Thrones look like? Remember the Emerald Tablet—the task of human beings is to imitate combining the heavenly with the earthly. Well, the supercollider may be a kind of wheel of creation, but I do not think that this is the right direction, but rather taking matter apart instead of participating in the action of creation. For an instance which provides an image of imitation of activity of the Thrones, I first have to go to Tibet. Recently, a certain Dr. Jarl (M.D.) reported, and supposedly video–taped, the following scene of a group of monks in Tibet. The monks were about the task of building a wall on the side of a steep cliff, 250 meters above the ground. They did not carry the stones up the side of the cliff. Instead, on the ground before them lay a smooth flat stone with a depression in its center, one meter across by 15 centimeters deep. A stone block of about 1x2 meters was put in the "bowl." At a distance of 63 meters from the bowl, 19 musical instruments (ragdongs) were placed side by side in a 90 degree arc. The instruments consisted of 13 drums and 6 trumpets. Eight of the drums were 1 meter wide and 1.5 meters long. Four were medium–sized, 0.7 by 1 meter, and one was small, 0.2 by 0.3 meters. The priest who stood behind the small drum gave the signal to start. The instruments made a loud noise and the monks sang a mantra. The stone started to sway. Then the block shot upward with increasing speed. Three minutes later it landed on the platform up on the side of the mountain. Within an hour it was possible to lift five or six stones up to the 250 meter level in a 500–meter–long parabolic curve. Could this not be a kind of communication between the monks and the Thrones, a prayerful working with the beings of matter?

I began with the issue of ecology; I do not believe we will get anywhere until we have a completely new view of matter, of the heavenly within matter and of the matter–creating within the heavenly. We will then need a physics which works this way, producing a spiritual technology that does things in the world as praise to the angels. This is not far–fetched, nor is it pure fantasy. I can name a dozen scientists who have worked this way, and whose efforts have all uniformly been suppressed. I am thinking of and remembering the following: Nikola Tesla, genius of electricity, whose knowledge of transmitting electricity through the earth was suppressed because it would make electric power available at no cost; Ruth Drown, who could take pictures of internal organs, diagnose, and treat physical diseases over distance through radionics. Her writings and pictures are available, as well as records of countless healings. She was brought into court and banned from practice; Samuell Hahnemann, founder of homeopathy, which I consider work with the creating beings within every substance in the world. His medicine was outlawed in 1910; Wilhelm Reich, discoverer of orgone energy, sent to prison by the U.S. government; Victor Schauberger—the Austrian water wizard, he was called—who discovered the spiral flow of water as an inexhaustible source of energy. He died in Germany after spending time in a U.S. government prison camp in Oklahoma, from which he had been released after turning over all his documents to the government; John Keely, who discovered how to obtain energy from the air. These people, among many others, I consider as those who worked with the angels and as such were a threat to the materialist world. Angels are practical. Are we now ready to ask for their help?

WHAT IS AN ANGEL?

PACO MITCHELL

The idea of an angel has a long history in human affairs, but as with most of the sacred images of our tradition, our tendency to literalize and concretize these images has had a hardening effect on them. The angel falls from the imagination from sheer weight, and we lose the symbolic sense of what must have been real and convincing experiences at one time.

During the last fifteen years the question of the angel has re–asserted itself as a concern of mine. In my therapy practice, in my own dreams, in synchronistic events, in the sculpture studio and as a flamenco guitarist, the cumulative impact of many experiences has forced me to recover the angel as a living psychic reality, a necessary feature of the soul, and a crucial factor in individuation.

So what is an angel? The traditional image that we are all familiar with is a fruitful starting point: *a human being with wings*. It lives with God and does his bidding for Him, exists in large numbers ("multitudes"), and can appear to humans both as a messenger from the divine realm and as a participant in human affairs.

Psychologically, the image of *human body* and *animal wings* suggests a fusion of two levels of being simultaneously, the animal–instinctual and the human–cultural realms meeting and sharing a moment of immediate presence. C. G. Jung may have been referring to something like this in *Psychological Types*[1] where he speaks of "creative fantasy," which he compares to the *spiritus phantasticus* of the Latin writer Synesius, who said, "The fantastic spirit is the medium between the eternal and the temporal, and *in it we are most alive*." (Emphasis mine.) Jung continues: "It unites the opposites in itself; hence it also participates in instinctive human nature right down to the animal level, where it becomes instinct and arouses daemonic desires . . . ."

To be able to hold one's daemonic desires and spiritual illuminations together in a moment of contained equilibrium is no small feat and without a doubt produces a state of extraordinary consciousness. It may be worth emphasizing that this "feat" is only in part an accomplishment of the ego; it depends primarily on the operation of an autonomous factor which transcends the ego. Synesius thus is forced to speak of a "spirit" as if speaking of a *person* with whom the ego interacts.

This experience is well known to artists, who commonly realize that their productions rely in high degree upon factors they cannot precisely control but upon which (upon whom?) they ultimately depend. Furthermore, in submitting to the creative process they expose themselves to often perilous psychological extremes. A satisfying work of art usually manages to balance those extremes to some extent.

Wings also denote a spiritual function: whatever is winged has a possibility of rising "above" the level on which humans are destined to live. The upwardness or verticality implied by wings is symbolically necessary to indicate that the plane of ordinary consciousness is being surpassed. Sometimes this takes the form of thoughts and intuitions which exceed our normal limits and abilities in moments of unusual clarity or vivid insight. From this perspective *we* have not thought brilliantly; rather, *the angel* has brought us a shining illumination. Jung's insistence on the autonomy and objectivity of thoughts, which he learned from his own spiritual guide Philemon, may apply here. In fact, the whole story of Jung and Philemon may be taken as one example of the encounter with an angel.

The "wings" of the angel may also carry us into an unusual *emotional* state. Anyone who has experienced that clear and steady passion that comes with a deep acceptance of the totality of one's being, wherein one *sees* the "rightness" of things—in Jungian terms, perhaps, a state of relatedness to the Self—could be said to be witnessing the presence of an angel. It can be like an animal awareness, a wordless readiness in the face of what is, what James Hillman calls "animal faith," what the Japanese call "muga" or one–pointedness. It is a state of equilibrium between the upward movement of "daemonic" desires and the downward movement of "light." *In it we are most alive.*

When an angel "appears" to a human being, we might say that a transcendant factor from the archetypal (heavenly) realm has manifested at the threshold of ego–consciousness. It is a "liminal" event (*limen* = threshold); it *happens to* the ego in a state of liminal or peripheral awareness (that state of mind so often courted by the creative artist). It is an agent of the Self (= agent of God, it does God's bidding). Furthermore, it has a message for the ego (our word "angel" derives from the Greek *angelos*, messenger), thus serving as a communicative link between ego and Self, man and God, temporal and eternal. Embodying as it does the relationship between man and God, it personifies that relationship and gives a face to one's destiny.

Taken in this light, as a moment of contact between archetypal contents/energies and the ego, it is a matter of no small importance whether the ego is strong enough to withstand the "messenger," let alone register the event in conscious memory, "hear" the message and translate it into human terms, and carry out the implications within one's own life. We have only to recall Jacob's struggle with the angel and his subsequent injury to remind ourselves that an encounter with archetypal energy is not exactly a picnic. Jung refers to it as a "bare–knuckled" event.

On the other hand, the appearance of an angel—in dreams, for example—announces a healing possibility, a link to the Self that would ease the neurotic disunion. Ironically the angelic figure is often the thing that is most feared. Sometimes it is an animal that appears, sometimes a human, sometimes it transforms from one into the other. When one is too impressed with one's own fear, their dream figure seems even more menacing. Too often the outcome is to flee or even to try to kill the "threatening" image. The dreamer would rather kill or avoid the messenger than hear from the inner Other.

If we can let the image speak, however, as in an active imagination, it may transform to reveal the deeper aspects of its nature and, surprisingly, *its need!* It challenges us and makes demands precisely because it needs something from us. William Blake hints at this when he says: "Eternity is in love with the productions of Time." Henri Corbin refers to the "angel of individuation," telling us that the angel's individuation comes first, *then* ours. And in *Answer to Job,* Jung stresses the crucial role of human consciousness in the divine drama, saying in effect that God needs man in order to evolve.

The angel can be seen as an expression of God's need to individuate, as it were, through contact with human consciousness. It is part of the self–regulating tendency within the individuating psyche, a necessary communication among parts of a whole, a glimpse of the spirit of the whole. It occurs at the imaginal level of the human–animal soul, whether as inward vision or outer synchronistic event. To carry an awareness of this level of psychic reality and to respond to it in some appropriate manner may well be a crucial task, not only for the fate of the individual but possibly at collective levels of human life as well. Blake calls it "winged Life." Our lives may well depend on its well–being.

ANGELS AND SCIENCE

ANGELS AND THE EVIDENCE OF THINGS NOT SEEN

DONALD COWAN

S cience, or perhaps I should say science of the past four centuries, has concerned itself with phenomena that are reproducible. A certain set of conditions will eventuate in another certain set of conditions infallibly, any time, for any observer—or so, at least, modern science has supposed. If this supposition does not hold, then it is assumed that some pertinent condition must have been omitted from the description of the original set or else that the phenomenon is of no concern to science. As corollary to the qualifying condition, science supposes that a rational connection exists between any two coupled events, the connection consisting of natural laws and logical deductions. Eventually, so this world view suggests, all events are interconnected by a great web of rationality, firmly anchored in measurable observables.

Such a deterministic picture of reality leaves little room for angels to get about. In actuality, however, the outlook of science has never been quite so deterministic as this enlightened ideal would have it. Biology hardly corresponds to it; and physics, which at the beginning of this century seemed on the verge of realizing the totally rational model, found it necessary, in the very search for its completion, to loosen the reins of reason. The imagination, it turns out, has an active role to play in science; and soaring in its thrust even beyond images, becomes in quantum mechanics pure intellection, based on faith in a mere analogue of rationality. Thus, what we might call imageless imagination has proved to be a necessary mode of thought in the understanding of elementary particles.

Modern science, accordingly, offers a respectable menu of entities that we can believe to exist without ever having observed them; we can either imagine or argue their reality. I call this action "not–seeing" the entity. This capability for not–seeing a particular entity depends very much on the culture in which it occurs: modern man can no more not–see an angel than medieval man could not–see an electron. Angels have been deleted from our available memory bank—at least until quite recently, I should say, and it is no doubt time to remove the constraints placed upon our sensibilities by enlightened rationalism.

If we are to construct a new angelology, we can begin with an old definition. An angel is an incorporeal intellect—a spirit without a body. My immediate reference is Mortimer Adler's book *Angels and Us*, a well–researched, carefully constructed account of traditional angelology with some critical up–dating. I recommend the book as a dispassionate introduction to angelology. Adler sets out to show that, whether or not they exist in actuality, minds without bodies are a philosophic possibility. If there are other compelling reasons to suppose that angels exist, he would say, then their being incorporeal intellects is no count against them. Adler distinguishes between philosophical and theological arguments about angels, philosophy looking to rationality for authority, theology looking to revelation. *Theologically* we can say that angels are *creatures*, created by God, and serving as His messengers. They are present in both Old and New Testaments and in the Koran, as guides, helpers, powers, announcers, guardians, adversaries, comforters. Their being creatures leaves open whole sets of questions for legitimate speculation within the constraints of Scriptures, since these are on the theological branch of the logos.

The *incorporeality* of angels opens another set of questions, these being on the philosophic branch, not constrained by Scripture. In my own set of analogies, I have said that angels are like photons—massless and indistinguishable, not observing an exclusion principal. Accordingly, as many as care to can dance on a pinhead. Adler says, on the contrary, that "though angels generally have no location, when on a mission they occupy the target locus 'intensively' and therefore exclusively"—one pin, one angel. This question hardly represents, however, as he acknowledges, the general tenor of learned inquiry concerning angels.

Traditional angelology has considered other, more serious, issues, theological and philosophic. Some of them have been the subject of pronouncements by Church Councils. (See Jean Daniélou, *The Angels and Their Mission*, for the traditional teachings of the Church Fathers concerning angels.) Why, then, do we need a new angelology? In all likelihood we do not actually *need* one. But we can say, with the displaced Lear, "Oh reason not the need." Angels add immensely to the opulence of existence; speculating and theorizing about them enhance the enjoyment of our own mortality. Delight, joy, or just plain fun and games, as in the head–of–a–pin query, is one reason, but there are others. In recent years the store of metaphors provided by science has increased the eligible descriptions for insights, so that we are, in a sense, *commissioned* to reconsider the dimensions of reality.

Let us take, as an example, some of the current thinking of cosmogonists. The stories they spread before us are myths, of course, and, like all myths, the actions they portray are hidden behind a veil that can be penetrated only by our imaginations. We all know portions of the present–day myth because it belongs to us who live in the culture for which it is produced. The Big Bang we more or less accept as the beginning of things some twelve to fifteen billion years ago. Stephen Hawkings' neat little book, *A Brief History of Time, from the Big Bang to Black Holes*, has had an immense popularity. Hawkings is that strange defiant British genius dying of Lou Gehrig's disease, unable to walk or even talk, punching out his thoughts on a computer. His account is profound if simple. A shorter version, Victor Weisskopf's article in the February 16 [1989] *New York Review of Books*, synthesizes in popular form the work of what he calls the Four Apostles of Genesis—the Britisher Hawkings, two Americans, and a Russian. I dare to recount an even more simplified story than Weisskopf's, the validity of which I would not defend at every point, though it is true to the findings of science in general and to our sense of the awesomeness of myths of creation.

In the beginning there was nothing—no space, no time, no light or energy—nothing. (Weisskopf calls it a true vacuum.) Nonetheless it burbles with expectation, fluctuating with half–quanta of all sorts, always adding up to zero—to nothing. Somewhere, sometime in this vast, timeless, spaceless void, the fluctuations result in a small, false vacuum—still nothing, but having the capacity for containing energy, expressible as a unified force once space exists. A fluctuation then appears as energy in this false vacuum and immediately forms an infinitesimal space which, because of its energy density, is incredibly hot, making of the false vacuum an expanding, true vacuum. The little space would disappear within the constraints of the indeterminacy principle except that, in this unique instance, the expansion cools it to an extent that gravity breaks free of the unified force, establishing negative (potential) energy and releasing positive (heat) energy, still totaling zero. The positive energy increases the rate of expansion so that the space again cools, causing the unified force to break apart into the strong and the electro–weak forces, repeating the whole procedure, as it does again when the electro–weak forces separate. All this happens in a millionth of a second—since time has now begun—and space has expanded to be very large and still very hot—some ten million degrees. Quarks and anti–quarks, leptons and their anti–mates have been formed from this heat energy, and that stage of creation is over.

With the unified force now completely broken into its four components—gravity, electro–magnetism, weak force, and strong force—the increasing expansion rate ceases. The space continues to expand, but now at a decreasing rate because of the pull of gravity. And of course it continues to cool, allowing matter, in various steps, to congeal and become what we see it to be.

I won't belabor the story, but three points can be made of it for our present purposes. Creation occurs *ex nihilo*—out of nothing, in good orthodox fashion. Energy, electric charge, matter are all created to be as much plus as minus so that they total zero at the beginning of things; but some asymmetry in the annihilation–creation process allows matter to dominate and anti–matter to disappear, except when called up in pair production. In any event, creation *ex nihilo* is the first point I want to preserve. It is scientifically as well as theologically sound.

The spiritual substance of which angels are constituted would also have been made *ex nihilo* and in plus and minus varieties. This substance is not fundamentally energy as is the e=mc^2 stuff of which we are made, and hence angels are not subject to gravity nor limited by the speed of light as we are. It is not physically necessary nor theologically sound to suppose that the fallen angels (the demonic powers), in a parallel to anti–matter, are composed of anti–spiritual substance. All angels, so this argument agrees, were made of the same good stuff, and Lucifer and his cohorts fell of their own free will. It seems likely that some asymmetry, some bias toward the good, has diminished the negative spiritual substance, so that the orders of angels can exist, in the same way that matter has prevailed over anti–matter in the physical universe.

The second point in this creation myth which we need to note has to do with the veil that I suggested hides the origins of myth. Weisskopf tells us that space wherein the temperature is above a thousand degrees K is opaque to light—I suppose because matter is there substantially a plasma of electrons and ions, minus and plus charges that cancel electromagnetic waves. The universe did not cool down to a thousand degrees until three hundred thousand years after the Big Bang; so whatever happened before that time is not visible to us—its light signals are blocked by the plasma—however sensitive we might make our instruments. Not being able to see or to know, we are free, then, to imagine and to postulate anything we choose in order to account for what goes on behind that veil, physically and spiritually, provided that what these postulates predict to emerge from behind the veil matches what is actually observed on this side of it. This method of conjecture, this wild sort of freedom, is legitimate for scientists and is available to us neophyte angelologists.

The third point to consider is that original void, that nothingness out of which the world was made. Though filled with energy in its various forms, the void is not abolished; the universe is still penetrated by it, whatever it is. It is not illegitimate to think of it as a spiritual reality—this nothingness—which resists all our measurements but which coexists with the observable universe. Angels, being incorporeal, might get around easily in it, able to transpose instantly to any target locus, according to their mission.

The commission for a new angelology extends beyond new metaphors that science or poetry provides to the universalizing of insight that has come about in our time. Spiritual presences such as angels in other lands, times, and cultures, we now realize, are not simply *like* our own but indeed *are* our own, requiring us not so much to amalgamate as to reconsider and reshape the cosmic form of our understanding. What are the angels of Indonesia, for example, how like, how different from those of the West? How can we unify all these signals from the spiritual inner space that permeates all existence? The angels are indeed cosmic, however parochial our own conceptions. We need to encompass those other angels, wherever we find them.

Along with the expanding of metaphors and the broadening of cultures, angelology can do with some reshaping in organization, more in accord with our present sensibility. Some democratization may be called for. "All angels are created free and equal," we might start, though we need to remember, perhaps, that Lucifer may already have tried that one. Perhaps there is a kind of equality possible among angels that does not lead to overweening pride. At any rate, the hierarchical notion of choirs may not be the most congenial to us today. The ranking of the choirs and the names used to designate them occur in Scripture but never, Adler reminds us, in any one place. Dionysius the Areopagite set the order forth as seraphim, cherubim, thrones—dominions, virtues, powers—principalities, archangels, angels—three hierarchies of three choirs each. His explication of assigned missions for the separate choirs was generally accepted by medieval theologians because supposedly he had been instructed by St. Paul at the time of his conversion on the Areopagus in Athens. It turns out, however, that his writings were six centuries or so later than the real Areopagite, Dionysius, the first Bishop of Athens; so I suspect some leeway is available to us—including, I say a little nervously, the question of species that Aquinas settled. Dominicans—and Thomas Aquinas was a Dominican—teach that one angel is as different from another as a cat is from a dog; I suspect that Aquinas's use of species is misinterpreted. By species, Adler notes, is meant ideas—that is, angels differ from one another in innate or infused knowledge: that is how they are individual, as persons are among mortals. No cats and dogs there.

Actually I am uncomfortable with the great chain of being notion of a single line of angels from here to eternity, ordered strictly according to their degrees of knowledge. Our thinking today tends more toward discrete states of being than toward a continuum. I suppose I am proposing that we suspend scholastic thought in reconsidering angelology until we again get a sense of the actual presence of angels, a certainty of their nearness. The reality of the angels needs to be felt before the schematism is established. Angels are known by the effects they leave behind. Rarely are they seen, and then only in retrospect. "Oh, that was an angel!"

Most often angels do not appear. We almost see them . . . if we had turned our heads a little faster. The whoosh that comes in the door, the light that effulges, the voice that speaks, all, all are of spiritual substance. If we are to make friends with angels, we must cultivate the faculty of almost–seeing. Sir Arthur Clutton–Brock tells of being in the Maritime Alps one June and discovering a spring in the shade of a sweet chestnut tree on the southern slope of a mountain:

> Then I knew suddenly how southern peoples had come by their myth of the water nymphs. Standing myself in the blazing sunlight, I almost saw a water nymph among the waters of that shade. . . . It was not the legend of the water nymph that brought her to my mind. It was the life and beauty of the stream that almost brought her to my eyes. The stream seemed so clearly to be occupied with a lovely, friendly business of its own that I almost saw a lovely friendly creature doing it. (B. H. Streeter, ed., *The Spirit*)

Almost–seeing and not–seeing are traditional ways of apprehending the spiritual depth of the world about us. It is the loss of this ability to "not–see" that troubles the speaker in John Crowe Ransom's "Persistent Explorer," on whose "literal ear" falls the sound of water. It teases him with the sense of a presence beyond the "simple physical water" which his eye and his ear confirmed. The thunder of the water falling

> . . . smote him somewhat as the loud
> Words of the god that rang around a man
> Walking by the Mediterranean.
> Its cloud of froth was whiter than the cloud
>
> That clothed the goddess sliding down the air
> Unto a mountain shepherd, white as she
> That issued from the smoke refulgently.
> The cloud was; but the goddess was not there.
>
> Deafening was the sound, but never a voice
> That talked with him; spacious the spectacle
> But it spelled nothing; there was not any spell
> Whether to bid him cower or rejoice.

The "pilgrim" Ransom describes makes no outcry; he manages only a "rueful grin." But he decides to "throw this continent away / And seek another country . . . " the voice of the disillusioned modern, seeking a new myth other than the myth of fact and the limited perception it allows.

Goddesses and fairies and angels come into our awareness from extended perception—from a spiritual contemplation of the things of this world, submitted to in their fullness, rather than from arid speculation. The construction of angelic forms by which angelic presences may be discerned requires the imagination and faith of several generations. As one commentator has said, "As vivid as some of these angel images may have been centuries ago, the process of building up angel forms today has all but disappeared." (Don Gilmore, *Angels, Angels Everywhere*.) We have to learn all over again to see, as Blake put it, "eternity in a grain of sand, heaven in a wild flower," to wait for what Sylvia Plath calls "a trick of radiance" that precedes "the long slow descent of the angel." We have to learn all over again to contemplate the sensuous world so that angels may invest our intuition with insight. We can then incarnate insights into images of materiality; but of themselves, insights are formed out of nothingness. They come into being out of that all–pervading spiritual nothingness that was here before we late–comers, angels as well as men, messed it up with our spaciness.

These angels belong to this creation; hence, in a special way, they belong to us. If there are further universes, as Stephen Hawkings and others suppose, let them have their own angels; there is plenty of nothing to go around.

ANGELS: THE MISSING LINK

LARRY DOSSEY

There is a widespread perception that angels in this day and age are nothing more than a benign metaphor, and that to believe in them is a harmless superstition. I believe this is not the case. I want to begin by relating an incident which convinces me that perceptions of angels still have real effects in the world—and that, on occasions, they are hardly benign.

I was working in the coronary care unit several years ago in a major Dallas hospital when I received an emergency call from a doctor in a small East Texas hospital, saying that he had transferred a patient of his to me via ambulance. The man was in serious trouble and had nearly died. The patient—I'll call him Joe—was a middle-aged East Texas farmer who had been hospitalized earlier that morning with chest pain. They hooked him up, as we say, and for a while Joe did just fine. Then something bizarre happened: he saw an angel. Now, Joe was about as unlikely a person to see an angel as anyone I can think of. He was hardly saintly, believe me. Anyway, as he recounted it, the angel, which was entirely black, hovered around the ceiling of his room in the coronary care unit and said, "Joe, you've been a good person, but now it's time for you to come home. I'm going to flutter down and touch you on the chest with my wing. When I do, you're going to come with me." Well, Joe was really scared and had no desire to "go home" with the black angel. He considered his options, which were not many. He tried to bargain but the angel could not be dissuaded. Wanting to know what effect the angel might be having on him, Joe craned his neck and followed the pattern of his heartbeat on the heart monitor on the wall, which was slightly behind him. It was steady and regular. Then, with one eye on the monitor and one on the angel, he saw the angel flutter down. When it touched him on the chest with his black wing, as he put it, "Doc, all hell broke loose. My heartbeat went crazy. I passed out; and when I woke up every doctor and nurse in East Texas was by my bedside, pounding on my chest!" Joe had suffered ventricular fibrillation, which is fatal if not treated immediately. Fortunately he was resuscitated by the skilled East Texas medical personnel, after which he was very much in favor of being transferred. After being admitted to the big hospital in Dallas, he did well. He seemed quite relieved to get out of East Texas and into one of the major Dallas hospitals, which have never been known for being overly infested with angels.

Having introduced the idea that the perception of angels can indeed have biological effects, I now want to attempt something that may sound heretical or blasphemous. I want to try to combine the concept of angels with that of modern evolutionary science—admittedly at the risk of offending both biological scientists on the one hand, and "angel–ologists" on the other.

If we could legitimately "angelify" the theory of evolution, it might indeed be a good thing to do in some ways. For I suspect Martin Lings may be right when he says, "[M]ore cases of loss of religious faith are to be traced to the theory of evolution . . . than to anything else."[1] The reasons are by now known by everyone. Darwin's theory of evolution has given us a not very flattering way of looking at ourselves. For example, in his book *Culture and Practical Reason*, Marshall Sahlins said, "We are the only people who think themselves risen from savages; everyone else believes they descended from gods."[2] But Sahlins is not quite right, for we have said that our origins are even more primitive than savages—we rose from apes, and from even more primitive life forms before that, which were themselves formed from the lifeless stuff of the universe: the atoms and subatomic particles whose behavior is regulated by the blind, meaningless laws of nature.

But we are not here to pillory Darwin. Anyone who speaks of his theory must, I believe, confess an immense debt to the man. It is a measure of his genius that his ideas could command almost total allegiance from scientists a century after his death. But like all theories that have demolished their opposition, Darwin's theory has become stultifying, and today it actively discourages many scientists from looking further into the nature of human origins.

In spite of this, however, criticism of Darwin abounds today. Some of it is eloquent, and some of it is superficial. The latter usually comes from religious fundamentalists and creationists who are fond of questioning, for example, the accuracy of methods central to the work of evolutionary biologists, such as carbon–fourteen dating techniques—areas in which most of them have not the slightest competence. Some of the most eloquent rebuttals to Darwin come from within biology itself. One of the best can be found in an article entitled "Mutiny on *The Beagle*," by Andrew P. Smith, a molecular biologist at the University of California at San Francisco.[3] There are also some highly readable critiques of evolutionary theory written by nonscientists for laypersons. Among the best are Arthur Koestler's *Janus: A Summing Up*[4] and philosopher of religion Huston Smith's *Beyond the Post–Modern Mind*.[5]

Just as a reminder, the theory maintains that living creatures evolve because of the action of natural selection, or pressures from the environment, working on chance genetic mutations. Those creatures which are "most fit" with regard to environmental pressures will produce more offspring; their genes will be perpetuated, and whatever forms or capacities they may possess will endure. Central to this process is the concept of chance and randomness. The mutations in the DNA of living things admit to no reason or purpose. This idea was summarized by the molecular biologist Jacques Monod: "The cornerstone of scientific method is . . . the systematic denial that 'true' knowledge can be got at by interpreting phenomena in terms of . . .'purpose.'"[6] There are problems with this. There are no criteria for what "the fittest" means other than "that which survives." So the theory is circular. As the eminent biologist, the late Professor C. H. Waddington put it, "Survival . . . denotes nothing more than leaving most offspring. The general principle of natural selection . . . merely amounts to the statement that the individuals which leave most offspring are those which leave most offspring. It is a tautology."[7]

Coupled with the tautology is the concept of chance, which by definition has no explanation. This led Huston Smith to remark, "A theory that claims to explain while standing with one foot on a tautology and the other in an explanatory void, is in trouble."[8] Arthur Koestler has gone so far as to call neo–Darwinism a "citadel in ruins."[9] Professor Pierre Grassé, who for thirty years held the chair for evolution at the Sorbonne, is likewise stern in his criticism. In referring to a problem that also troubled Darwin—how random mutations could lead to the formation of an organ as complex as the eye—he states, "There is no law against daydreaming, but science must not indulge in it."[10]

Why does the theory endure if these problems are obvious? Ludwig von Bertalanffy, originator of the theory of natural systems, put it this way: "I think the fact that a theory so vague, so insufficiently verifiable and so far from the criteria otherwise applied in 'hard' science, has become a dogma, can only be explained on sociological grounds."[11]

The book of proof of evolution is the fossil record—the bones and the preserved remnants of creatures of long ago. It was originally felt by Darwin and his successors that when enough fossils had been assembled one could observe a gradual and unbroken lineage of living things, beginning with primitive forms and ending with the most complex. A problem, however, is that the fossil record has enormous gaps and discontinuities in it. This gave rise early on to the concept of "missing links"—fossils which, when found, would prove beyond a shadow of a doubt the gradual development of more complex forms through time. But today the missing links have not been found, and the gaps remain. It is now generally conceded that missing links between most species will not be found. The changes seemed to have happened too fast, and were too "jumpy"—so jumpy that the original theory of gradualism has been challenged by a new theory put forth by biologists Stephen Jay Gould and Niles Eldrige, called "punctuated equilibrium."[12]

What about angels? Where do they fit in, if anywhere? In speaking of them, I want to regard them much as did St. Thomas, who saw them as filling the gap between man and God in the hierarchy of being. I am not interested in whether he was right in regarding them as wholly distinct orders of beings just as real, or more so, than ourselves. I would like to playfully designate angels as a kind of missing link in the origins of humankind.

How might angels be a missing link? It is helpful to recall that all esotericism subscribes to the idea that reality is hierarchical, or made up of successively higher levels of reality. These levels reach from the lowest material plane of subatomic particles and atoms to the ultimate spiritual realization. A familiar term describing this span is the universal Great Chain of Being, a term popularized by Arthur Lovejoy in his book of the same name, in which he states, "The conception of the universe as . . . ranging in hierarchical order from the meagerest kind of existents . . . through 'every possible' grade up to the *ens perfectissimum* . . . has, in one form or another, been the dominant official philosophy of the larger part of civilized mankind through most of its history."[13] The key point is that reality is tiered, and that "being" increases as one ascends the Great Chain. ("Ascend" is used figuratively; no up or down, or any spatial direction, is involved.)

What does it mean to say that "being increases or decreases" at different hierarchical levels? This depends on several factors, according to Huston Smith, among which are (1) power, (2) duration, (3) locale, (4) unity, and (5) worth. For instance, if something has infinite power, duration that is eternal, a locale that is omnipresent, is undivided, and possesses ultimate worth, it would be absolute. This would correspond to the highest point on the Great Chain of Being, or God.[14]

Now, it is universally recognized that a hierarchy exists also in the material world. Some of the levels are the subatomic, atomic, molecular, and cellular. As one moves higher one sees levels of increasing sophistication in living things: organs, organ systems, whole bodies, species, family units, cultures, nations, etc. Hierarchy, then, is not just a theological or religious idea; it is an accepted concept in modern science.

But what causes hierarchies to form in the biological world? Why do living things evolve from the simple to the complex? As we saw, evolutionists would respond with the usual explanation that environmental pressures cause the selection of certain complex traits that aid in eternal struggle to survive and produce offspring. Nothing more is required.

The answer given by all esoteric philosophies and most religions, however, is different. A *telos* is involved—a "push" or "pull," depending on one's viewpoint, which shapes and guides evolutionary development in a particular direction. This is what Aldous Huxley called the divine "tug" from in front.[15]

But the perennial philosophies do not stop with a telos. They assert that a process exists prior to evolution, called involution. When involution is completed, the stage is then set for evolution to begin. Some persons insist that the reason evolution seems to work as well as it does is that it is a precise, backward readout of the prior process of involution. In other words, evolution is simply following a blueprint or design already laid out.

The clearest description of this process can be found in Ken Wilber's remarkable book, *Up From Eden*.[16] Wilber has synthesized the concept of involution from Christian mysticism, Vedanta Hinduism, Mahayana Buddhism, and many other traditions. Let me illustrate this process by focusing on only one tradition, Vedanta Hinduism. According to this cosmology/psychology, the ultimate Brahman–Atman periodically, in the course of the Universe, "gets lost"—for the fun and the sport of it (called *lila*), seeing how "far out" it can get. In throwing itself outward and downward (again, no specific directions are implied), Spirit or the Godhead begins to manifest more and more objectively in the world. In this process, material substance eventually "precipitates" from Spirit in its simplest form, manifesting in the quantum/subatomic domain.

Because Spirit temporarily "forgets" itself and thus "loses" itself in successively lower levels, one sees with each descending level less and less consciousness. The Great Chain, then, begins with Spirit or superconsciousness and "descends" to simple consciousness and finally to subconsciousness. And, because each level has less consciousness than its predecessor, each level cannot consciously grasp or fully remember its origin. Thus, each level "forgets" its senior level.

There is a similar Christian concept to this process, called *kenosis*. "Kenosis" means approximately "self–emptying." Spirit creates the world by giving or emptying itself into and as the world, but without in any way ceasing to be itself. It is that an amnesis occurs, based on the forgetting of Spirit by Spirit.

To summarize: this whole "downward" movement is called involution, in which each level demonstrates (1) a successive "moving away" from the Godhead, (2) a successive lessening of consciousness, (3) a successive forgetting or amnesis, (4) a successive stepping down of Spirit, (5) a successive increasing of alienation, separation, dismemberment, and fragmentation, and (6) a successive objectification and dualism. But, importantly, the divorcement from Spirit is only illusory, for each level is still nothing but Spirit at play. Yet the agony of each level is that it appears or seems to be separated from Spirit—fallen and lost forever. But Spirit is not lost at each level, just forgotten; obscured, not destroyed; hidden, not abandoned. As Wilber says, this is a great game of hide–and–seek, with Spirit being It.[17]

Somewhere, then, between the Godhead and the final level of descent, is the angelic domain—a region not fully concretized and unconscious, but not fully the Godhead, either. Whatever angelic qualities there may be are enfolded in the lower reaches via the process of involution. And when this process is completed, the process of evolution—the backward readout of involution—is ready to begin. And as it does, eventually a point is reached when this enfolded angelic potential is made manifest once more, in man's evolutionary climb toward the Godhead.

There may be tremendous agreement between this view and much of evolutionary theory. We say today that the universe started with the Big Bang. Before this time there was "nothing there." From the point of view expressed above, there indeed was nothing material in existence before the start of the universe's evolutionary process—only nonmaterial, nonmanifest Spirit. After billions of years the physical universe appeared. As it did so, higher–order wholes gradually emerged *through* it. We have no trouble, from this perspective, saying that humans came through apes. The problem arises when we try to say we came from apes, or from matter only. This amounts to denying the prior process of involution, in which Spirit was enfolded in matter, and through which—not from which—it reappears as evolution proceeds.

It seems to me that to deny some prior process of involution gets us into some extraordinarily irrational positions. Without involution—or something like it—we cannot account for the appearance of consciousness. With involution, the appearance of consciousness is predicted. It appears automatically as evolution proceeds, because it was enfolded—or involuted—in matter from the beginning. Not admitting this, evolutionists have trouble explaining where consciousness came from. Some scientists admit this. Take the comment of Werner Heisenberg, who originated the Heisenberg Uncertainty Principle in quantum physics. He states, "There can be no doubt that 'consciousness' does not occur in physics and chemistry, and I cannot see how it could possibly result from quantum mechanics."[18] Or take the comments of Niels Bohr, whose name is virtually synonymous with modern physics: "We can admittedly find nothing in physics or chemistry that has even a remote bearing on consciousness."[19]

However, it must be said that most evolutionists blithely ignore the problem of how one could conceivably get consciousness out of dead atoms, or they accept poorly defined explanations. One of the favored "explanations" today is the theory of "emergence." According to this theory, consciousness "emerges" at a certain level of organizational complexity of the brain. But how? As Nobelist–neurophysiologist Sir John Eccles states, in all the laws of physics and chemistry, as currently understood, there is nothing whatsoever that refers to consciousness. And as philosopher of science Sir Karl Popper has stated, to say that consciousness "emerges" from matter amounts only to putting a question mark at a certain stage in evolution. Today the biologists' concept of emergence does not help us explain the origins of consciousness;

it has no more explanatory power than saying "Whatever happens, happens." This is not to deny that consciousness emerges, for it does; but it may do so, not from matter, as current "explanations" of emergence insist, but through matter.[20]

Another major hurdle for evolutionists is the general contention that consciousness is effete; that is, it really cannot "do" anything. "Mind over matter" is an absurdity, they say. But if it is effete and cannot "do" anything, why did it increase in the process of evolution? All evolutionists agree that "mind" has increased. But only that which aids survival by "doing" something in the world is selected and perpetuated, according to evolutionary theory. Accordingly, consciousness—if it cannot act in the world—should have died out long ago. On this point, the prior process of involution is helpful. Simply put, consciousness appears in the evolutionary process because it was there to begin with.

It is interesting to interpret some of our myths in the light of involution. According to this, the Fall began long before Adam and Eve left Eden. It began with the beginning of involution itself—when Spirit began its play of forgetting itself, long before the physical world manifested. By the time physical Eden was created, the forgetting of Spirit by Spirit was complete. On this account, all the romantic myths and theories of scholars who maintain that Eden was some sort of trans–personal Heaven where God and man were a blissful unity are wrong. Rather, it was a pre–personal realm of earth, nature, raw instinct, emotion, and unselfconsciousness. It was paradisiacal ignorance, not enlightenment, that prevailed. Full psychological and spiritual awareness still lay ahead in the future. As the Russian Christian mystic Nicolas Berdyaev stated, "Not everything was revealed to man in paradise, and ignorance was the condition of life in it. It was the realm of the unconscious."[21] With the eating of the Tree of Knowledge, man and woman realized they were mortal, largely unconscious, and separated from the Godhead—the awareness of which was experienced as pain and guilt. "They did not get thrown out of the Garden of Eden," Wilber states; "they grew up and walked out (. . . for this courageous act, we have Eve to thank, not blame.)"[22]

If we look back on evolution as the reversal of involution, the entire process may seem more intelligible. Involution is a process of dismemberment; evolution is a process of re–membership, in which we see the reappearance of higher–order wholes—which is what we indeed observe. Involution is a process of decreasing consciousness; evolution is a process of increasing consciousness—which, again, is what the data shows. And the driving force behind the entire process is the return of Spirit to Spirit—Spirit remembering and reconstituting itself—building bigger and better brains in living organisms in this process, through which it can manifest this remembering.

If the goal of evolution is to retrace the prior process of involution in a return to the Godhead, this is why man and woman had to leave Eden—not dwell there eternally as so many want to believe. Berdyaev, as Wilber points out, is one of the few theologians who has seen this. Berdyaev put it this way: "The myth of the Fall does not humiliate man, but extols him to wonderful heights. . . . The myth of the Fall is a myth of man's greatness."[23]

Of those who have described the *telos* driving evolution, Wilber lists many philosophers, including Aristotle, Aurobindo, Radhakrishnan, Chaudhuri, Gopi Krishna, Teilhard de Chardin, Fichte, Schelling, and Hegel—a lineage that includes East and West, ancients and moderns.

I want to end by saying that we are not obliged to accept without criticism all the officious pronouncements so frequently made by presumptuous scientists about the verdict being in when it comes to evolutionary theory. It isn't. As a single example, I shall refer to a recent paper by geneticist John Cairns of Harvard, "The Origin of Mutants," published in the prestigious journal *Nature*. "The purpose of this paper," Cairns stated, "is to show how insecure is our belief in the spontaneity (randomness) of most mutations. It seems to be a doctrine that has never been properly put to the test." Further, "The origin of genetic variation has been the subject of bitter controversy throughout the nineteenth century and into the first half of the twentieth. . . . At its extremes it was an argument between reductionists and romantics. . . . The early triumph of molecular biology strongly supported the reductionists. . . . Curiously, when we come to consider what mechanism might be the basis for the forms of mutation described in this paper we find that molecular biology has, in the interim, deserted the reductionist. Now almost anything seems possible."[24]

Somewhere, angels must be smiling.

Now, if the process of involution did occur, there should be traces of angels all about us—residue of these missing links between God and man. The question is, where is it, and why is it so hard to see? The answer may be that we have to know how to look—or listen, since the evidence of angels may be more acoustical than visual.

After all, one of the properties traditionally attributed to angels is music. We speak of the "angelic choirs," "angelic music" sung by the "angelic hosts," and make comments such as "she sings like an angel." There may be good reason for this. For, as strange as it may seem, if we look at DNA, the substrate on which the process of evolution operates, we can actually see the musical signatures of something—possibly angels.

The idea of relating DNA and music stems from the work of geneticist Susumu Ohno at the Beckman Research Institute of the City of Hope in Duarte, California, and is now a matter of record in the genetics literature.[25] In understanding Dr. Ohno's insight, remember that every organism's genes are composed of strands of DNA, which in turn are made up of four so-called nucleotides containing the nucleic acids adenine, guanine, cytosine, and thymine. In DNA, these "base pairs" combine with each other in regular sequences.

Dr. Ohno did something very creative: he assigned musical notes to these nucleotides—*do* to cytosine (C), *re* and *mi* to adenine (A), *fa* and *sol* to guanine (G), and *la* and *ti* to thymine (T). Now, having assigned musical notes to each base, Dr. Ohno found that the genes could be translated into music.

Interestingly, he found that the more evolved an organism is, the more complicated is the music. The DNA of a single–cell protozoan, for example, translates into a simple four–note repetition; as you march up the evolutionary ladder, things get more complex.

Dr. Ohno has notated fifteen songs of the DNA of living organisms during the past two years. He takes some liberties with the timing of the musical notes, the key in which the music is played, and the duration of each note. In order to fill out the harmonies, his wife, Midori, adds a few notes, and then the melodies are performed by professional musicians.

This procedure works in reverse, also. Not only can you make music starting with DNA, you can start with great pieces of music and describe what the DNA might look like by using the reverse process. When he transcribed a Chopin piece into a chemical notation, sections of the resulting formula were that of a human cancer gene. Even cancers have their own music—wonderful music, at that!

Have we found evidence for the "angelic missing link" in this music that can be derived from the DNA code itself? I leave it to your imagination to decide.

Many great artists, writers, and musicians have heard messages in nature, some of them musical. When Mozart heard a complex, lengthy piece of music fully formed, where was it coming from? When Hesse said, in the prologue to *Demian*, that he learned to listen to the messages his blood whispered to him, what was he actually hearing? What about synesthetes—those people who have multiple senses operating in situations where a single sense usually operates?—people, for example, who "hear" color or who "hear" smells? Are they in touch with some musical, angelic residue encoded in their own bodies?

If this speculation seems fanciful, we should recall that there is no reason in principle why DNA has to be described in the familiar alphabetical chemical symbols—C for carbon, N for nitrogen, etc. It could be described in many symbolic ways, not just alphabetically. If we were imaginative enough to think musically as well as alphabetically, this just might permit us to "hear the music," and might prevent us from using pejorative words like "dead," "purposeless," and "inert" in referring to the stuff that makes up our bodies.

Recognizing the music latent in DNA suggests a new way of looking at evolution. Rather than evolution being a way of passing genes from one generation to another, it could be a way of passing the music along—of one generation "making music" for the next. Mutations would be ways of tinkering with the melody, of creating new, more complex tunes. "Survival of the fittest" might mean something like "staying in key" or "maintaining the harmony."

But the material world is more than just DNA—it is plants, rocks, trees, even stars and galaxies. One could conceivably notate any of these things musically. When Boethius spoke of "the music of the spheres," was he comprehending this sort of notation in the heavens? Was he actually hearing the angels sing?

There are other worlds that await us, worlds that can become visible—and audible—by a creative act of the imagination.

Some of these worlds are musical.

They may even be angelic.

Angels from the Time to Come

Frederick Turner

Certain moments in a good story possess a quality that is logically very strange indeed, and which renders them often haunting and unforgettable. Consider Dorothea's choice of Ladislaw as her lover in *Middlemarch*: the logic of fiction would dictate that Dorothea should pair up with Lydgate, who is a heavyweight like her, and if after reading the first half of the book we were to try to predict the outcome, this would probably be our choice. On the other hand, when she upsets our expectations we are on reflection not disappointed but deeply excited by the depth of what has happened: strangely, we now realize that Dorothea's surprising choice was really inevitable all along, that it had to be that way; her originality, her tenderness, her St. Teresa–like sense of mastery could express itself no other way.

We get the same feeling when Edmund has his deathbed repentance in *King Lear*, and even more so when it turns out that his repentance, which would be the perfect *deus ex machina* to save Cordelia's life, ends up with no apparent plot function at all: in fact it makes Cordelia's death even more unexpected, arbitrary, and horrifying. Yet we recognize immediately the absolute rightness of this reversal; it was inevitable all along!

One could cite dozens of other examples: the *Odyssey* is a compendium of them, Faulkner is a master at the art, and so is Tolstoy. In music the same thing happens: Mozart will often pile two or three twists of melodic or harmonic surprise upon each other, and yet in retrospect the structure of his piece will hold firm, perfectly braced, airy, yet as strong as adamant.

The peculiar thing about such moments is that, by their unpredictability before the event combined with their retrodictability after it, they radically defy the requirement that truth be independent of time; and yet they are by no means arbitrary or merely expedient—it is not as if the artist were irresponsibly flinging in extraneous incidents or distorting the integrity of the work by arbitrary crowd–pleasing interventions. It was Plato who most clearly established the idea that truth cannot trim its sails with the winds of time, that two and two must equal four for all eternity, not just today, or on Wednesdays, or in the past but not the future. Certainly there are kinds of coherent truth of which Plato's requirement of temporal indifference must hold. But he is perhaps wrong in implying that coherence and intelligibility—which are supreme virtues, else we could not even reason about such matters, and must come to blows—are only possible under conditions of time invariance. Edmund and Dorothea and Odysseus and Quentin Compson and Anna Karenina are coherent and intelligible—so much so that a lifetime is not enough to appreciate how much. But much of what they do has the peculiar capacity to alter the past in such a way as to make certain futures inevitable, when they were not so before.

We need, then, a new logic to talk about such actions, one which always has two senses—a strong sense, which applies retroactively, and a weak sense, which applies prospectively. Recent developments in Italian philosophy have produced the expression "weak thought," which, though it properly applies to the level of assertion and probability in a proposition, can be used here as well. Researchers in cognitive science, the philosophy of mathematics, and artificial intelligence have all come to recognize that the work of the human mind cannot be modeled without some kind of soft linkage between concepts which relies on large vague databases, partial resemblances, and relative probabilities of truth. But what we want are laminated words, whose one face is weak and whose other is strong, and a reasonably rule–governed way of using them.

In the Oriental martial arts there is a fine practical vocabulary of concepts for dealing with such matters. A karate expert will view his or her opponent with "soft eyes," meaning that the attention is global rather than concentrated, and will achieve by this a decisive edge in speed over an opponent. But the martial arts vocabulary does not easily lend itself to philosophical speculation; and this essay is a kind of game or fiction in speculative philosophy. We can find in contemporary theoretical physics perhaps a more exactly defined set of terms—specifically, in John Archibald Wheeler's notion of the strong and weak anthropic principles. What this essay will do is explore some of the implications of the anthropic principle(s) for a subject, which, we will see, is in its essence bound up with time asymmetry: that is, the nature of angels.

A simple experiment will illustrate one of the most mysterious phenomena in quantum mechanics. Take two polaroid sunglass lenses and hold them against the light, one behind the other. If they are aligned so that their axes of polarization are parallel with each other, the two lenses together will let almost as much light through as one lens alone. But if you rotate one lens so that the axes of polarization are at an angle, the amount of light getting through will diminish until, when the lenses are at 90° to each other, no light gets through at all. A sunglass lens cannot bend the polarization of the light; all it can do is stop light which is vibrating in a north–south direction, say, and let light through that is vibrating in an east–west direction. Thus it makes perfect sense that the two lenses should together stop all the light, since all the directions in which light could vibrate involve some combination of north–south and east–west.

The mystery appears if we place a third lens at about 45° between the two lenses that have already been set at 90° to each other. Common sense would suggest that to do so would be a little superfluous, because all the light has already been stopped, and total darkness cannot be further darkened. What actually happens, though, is this: light now starts passing through the three lenses, when it could not pass through two!

What does this mean? Quantum physics offers various explanations, all of which involve some deep and beautiful violation of common sense. One goes like this: a wave (or particle) of light before it reaches the lenses does not "know" what its polarization is, and the first lens forces the light to "make up its mind." However, it only has to make up its mind about one of the axes of polarization, not any others. If the second lens it hits absolutely excludes what the first lens absolutely permitted (90°) then all light is stopped. This is proved by the fact that if the 45° lens is placed on either side of the pair of opposite lenses, and not between them, it cannot alleviate the darkness, because the unmediated contradiction still exists. But if the middle lens is at 45° to the others, the light gets to make up its mind again, and by the time it reaches the third lens it has "forgotten" about the "decision" it was forced to make at the first lens; the light coming through the second lens is just light that has been through a northeast–southwest filter, and that is all it is. The third lens does not absolutely contradict the second, and thus about one–fourth of the original light gets through.

But something very peculiar has happened to the nature of time in this account. Events and objects are constituted by the information that they exchange with other events and objects and with themselves; and the means by which that information gets exchanged are, as forms of light, subject to quantum uncertainty. Which means that when the light that tells us of events in the filament of a light bulb, or on the surface of the sun, is forced to declare the orientation of its vibration, then the nature of the lightbulb and of the sun becomes retroactively a little more definite. Reality is, when unobserved, only approximate in its nature: it is a probability function or "wave function" specifying a number of possible states which it might assume if challenged, at which time the packet of uncertainty that constitutes a particle before it is measured is "collapsed"—forced retroactively to make up its mind. Why "retroactively"? Because light, and any other form of information, is limited in the speed of its propagation, and anything we observe is already in the past of the observing eye.

Reality, then, depends partly on how we measure it. The two–lens system asks a different question of the world than the three–lens system, and thus the answer we get is different, and thus the reality of which we asked the question, and which is already in the past, must be different. Events do not occur in and of themselves, but exist in a kind of partnership with their observers. The "mighty world of eye and ear," as

Wordsworth puts it in *Tintern Abbey*, is made up of "what we half perceive, and half create."

Now this idea can be, and has often been, misinterpreted by those who through wishful thinking, or malicious mischief against the noble and simple authority of science, or a preference for the moral excitement of their own opinion over what is demonstrable, desire to discredit the possibility of reasonably sure knowledge. Hence the conclusion that some critics have drawn from a superficial study of quantum theory, that nature is incoherent and dependent upon the ideological views of scientists, which in turn reflect the political system and its entrenched power and privilege, etc. And thus such abominations as "Jewish science" in the thirties and "feminist science" now. The fallacy lies in the fact that the "observing" and "measuring" that collapses the wave function can be performed by other entities than human beings. A rock can collapse a photon's wave function too, and the universe had a definite being, though a simpler and cruder one, before human beings evolved. Thus the universe has been continually and cumulatively "making up its mind" through a consensus of exchange of information for fifteen billion years. We are now an increasingly important part of that consensus, but as Lysenko learned when his Communist wheat died in Siberia, politics cannot resist a sufficiently negative vote by the inanimate public of the universe. By the time we observe most things that are larger than subatomic particles, they are already part of a healthy, functioning, mutually–supporting reality system, to be altered only if we know the faultlines of its construction and have the technology to pry them apart.

Let us revise our earlier formula about the partnership of events and their observers, and say that events and objects at least need to be registered as such by some other event or object that has the selective sensitivity to do so. Many events and objects can be registered by very crude "observers" that need only be made of matter to do their job. Others, though—and here things get interesting—do need rather sophisticated observers; and there are many whose more complex aspects only come into existence at the call of such sophistication and sensitivity. Or let us put it this way—the observer is enfolded, in whatever way the observer is capable, in the being of the prior event that is observed. If the observer is crude, its report will form part of the brute consensus of matter; but if the observer is very sensitive, new properties will appear, and will really begin retroactively to exist, within the past event that is observed. Organized forms of matter are more sensitive, have finer resonances, than amorphous ones; living things, animals and plants and so on, are more sensitive than stones; and we are more sensitive than animals and plants, if only because our sensitivity includes theirs (and if it did not, we could not even argue about their relative merits).

It was Wheeler's idea to apply this reasoning to the most important quantum event of all: the origin of the universe. In what sense was the origin of the universe a "quantum event"? The Big Bang theory, which best satisfies the evidence, requires that before it was $1/10^{20}$ second old the whole of the universe must have been packed into a space less than $1/10^{10}$ centimeters in radius, and this was all the space there was. It is precisely this realm of space and time within which quantum theory holds, and within which the role of the observer becomes important. We human beings are certainly the most obvious and sensitive observers of the origin—for instance, we are still picking up the background radiation of the Big Bang from all directions, a form of information about it that is direct and unmediated, if very old.

One of the greatest challenges to the cosmologist is why the universe originated with the precise numerical constants that it did. These constants include the inverse square law by which the force of gravitation diminishes with distance, the speed of light, the electron volt constant, Planck's constant, and so on. If these constants had been different in the slightest degree, no conceivable form of life could have evolved; indeed it is hard to see how even organized matter could have evolved. Why should we have had the astonishing luck to have gotten the exact origin that would bring about a universe which in the fullness of time would deliver us into existence?

Wheeler's anthropic principle answers this riddle elegantly by suggesting that of all the possible origin–states for the universe, only one would bring about observers of it that could collapse its wave–function, ask it the question that would force it to declare a particular identity. Thus the universe originated as it did, with that particular set of constants, because it was since seen to do so. Any other hypothetical universe would remain only an eternal possibility. We, its observers, necessitated an observer–producing origin; and our question about it, like Parsifal's, though long delayed, transforms the Waste Land of the original uncertainty into the rich and productive field of cosmic evolution.

However, this formulation of the idea is still a rather coarse one. There is, as we have already noted, a wide range of organisms between photons and human beings, of varying degrees of organization and complexity; from atoms which are sensitive to electromagnetic and gravitational information, through crystals, which are also sensitive to vibration, heat, and so on, to animals which can smell, see, and hear. All of these can act as observers and ask, in their own way, the fructifying question of Parsifal. Thus it would be more accurate to say that as more and more sensitive observers evolved, they re–specified more and more exactly what the initial state of the universe must have been.

A later, more evolved and sophisticated organism collapses the wave function not only of the Big Bang but also of all prior organisms; either indirectly, through the Big Bang itself, or directly, because of its implicit observation of quantum events within those simpler, earlier beings. Thus the chordates had to be as they were to bring about vertebrate observers; vertebrates must be just so to occasion mammalian observers, mammals to bring about primates, and primates to be the ancestors of human beings. The fruit of any process is also an observer of it and thus a partial determiner of its nature.

Wheeler's anthropic principle, thus generalized, now seems to fit nicely our requirement for an intelligible account of time asymmetry. As we look forward toward a putative event we need assume no more than the weak anthropic principle: whatever that event, it will syllogistically bring about a plausible future observer of it (or else there would be no evidence that it had happened). As we look backwards we can assume the strong anthropic principle: that earlier event was partly necessitated by the requirement that it help produce a universe in which we can look back at it. And the weak and strong principles are not isolated from each other, but share a strange seam across their back sides, so to speak, and form a kind of Janus, a sort of transitional January between the old year and the new. Through that semipermeable seam there is a leakage or tunneling of implication or entailment, just as the present moment conducts and mixes the different logical environments of past and future into each other.

How strange this reasoning is! Indeed, before its logic unfolded, it would have been utterly implausible to the mind that now thinks it; and yet as each idea precipitates into being, it opens up a new landscape in whose context a new plausibility emerges. There must be something in it, so the mind reflects, for the process itself is so like the very story of real life!

For a new implication has just come over the horizon: our own nature and activity, as well as being partly determined by past causes, and partly the result of the autonomous self–organizing iterative feedback of our own consciousness, must also be subtly guided and conditioned by their own future observers. Our own wave function is being collapsed by future awarenesses that we will help to bring into being and which will in turn ratify our existence and help us to fall into a definitive shape.

I know perfectly well that my own mind is not capable in itself of those leaps or marvelous compactions into a new thought which it undergoes in the process of composing a poem or a creative essay. Perhaps this feeling itself, of there being some niche or prepared receptor for the heavy current of thought, some attractor that will emerge out of its turbulence, was what the Greeks meant by the Muse. Sometimes she speaks with unmistakable and imperious tongue (yet she is so delicate, so easily deniable, is she not?), sometimes in a still, small voice; but if one had never experienced her, and suddenly heard her voice for the first time, one would be convinced that one were in the presence of the supernatural, or that one were hallucinating thoughts not of one's own making. Only when she is, as she is, a daily source of insight and surprised reminder, do we take her voice as normal and unremarkable. But without it how dull and dim the world would be!

All cultures know of them, these spirits or kamis or "presences /
That piety, passion or affection knows," as Yeats put it in *Among School
Children*, these beautiful and terrible animate forms that visited Lot and
Abraham and Jacob and Ezekiel. The report of them is so widespread that
they must represent some reality. Let us name these future knowers of us,
these observer–participants in the creation and generation of our nature
and being. They are the angels.

But as the argument implies, they are not only the attractors and
subtle guides of our action, our creative evolution. They are also its result.
Angels are painted as babies, as putti: of course, because they are our children, our unborn descendants. Children; but evidently children winged
with incalculable power and complexity of purpose; as far beyond us as
we are beyond the dim wonderings of pithecanthropus; as they were
beyond the animals, plants, minerals, and physical particles that pre-
ceded them—those forerunners that, by observing, we lend a more distinct being:

> Frühe Geglückte, ihr Verwöhnten der Schöpfung,
> Höhenzüge, morgenrötliche Grate
> aller Erschaffung,—Pollen der blühenden Gottheit,
> Gelenke des Lichtes, Gänge, Treppen, Throne,
> Räume aus Wesen, Schilde aus Wonne, Tumulte
> stürmisch entzückten Gefühls und plötzlich, einzeln,
> Spiegel: die die entströmte eigene Schönheit
> wiederschöpfen zurück in das eigene Antlitz.

> Early successes, favorites of fond Creation,
> ranges, summits, dawn–red ridges
> of all forthbringing,—pollen of blossoming godhead,
> junctures of light, corridors, stairways, thrones,
> chambers of essence, shields of felicity, tumults
> of stormily–rapturous feeling, and suddenly, separate,
> mirrors, drawing up again their own
> outstreamed beauty into their own faces.[1]

Rilke on angels, repeating much that we know from Ezekiel and Blake and Giotto, and more strangely the ritual art of Indonesia and China and Tibet, the dragon–forms of Mayan vision–carvings, of African and Eskimo spirit–masks; the authentic voice of the shaman.

If the angels are our children, what must we do to bring them into being?—for clearly they are so beautiful that we ought to bring them into being. Having once experienced them, one can be in no doubt of the value of one's existence, could one have but the smallest role in opening to them the gates of history.

We are at a remarkable juncture in our own history and indeed of the history of the cosmos: when evolution becomes fully self–aware, when nature finds the theme and mode it has sought from the beginning. Not that the change that is coming will be utterly unprecedented. We have always been capable of directing our own evolution: in the traditional way, by choosing mates who have the beauty and wit and capacity for love and strength of mind that will lead the species by increments toward the more deeply human; and we know the more deeply human as horse breeders know racing temperament and apple breeders know a noble strain, even before we have good examples of what we are after. In like fashion a poet recognizes the line or cadence or image as truly part of the unborn poem. But now that process has become irretrievably self–conscious, and is assisted by a more and more powerful battery of technical aids.

However shocking and terrifying is the idea of biological engineering, we cannot now lay it aside. If we want angels, should we not build and beget them? Genes can be altered, added, removed; and, more excitingly, new studies show that we use only a tiny fraction of our DNA, and that our development and mature being depends almost as much on a unique pattern of suppression and expression of the genes we already have, as on what the genes are to begin with. This pattern itself may be subject to craft and sculpture. Especially in this area, now known as epigenetics, and encompassing the older, more empirical sciences of embryology and development, some of the ancient enemies of human-kind—cancer, aging, immune deficiencies, neurochemical diseases— now seem to be revealing their weaknesses.

Slowly, infinitely carefully, in fear and trembling, we will continue what we have already started: the correction of inherited diseases, the repair of genetic deficits, the tuning of the chemistry of mood, memory, and thought so as to express fully, rather than in its present muffled and crippled form, the special grandeur of each individual's inheritance. Those who are great artists, athletes, givers, scientists, lovers, know the sweet clarity and power of perfect work and action, in moments that are tragically brief but which nevertheless make a lifetime worthwhile. But they also know the stifling burden of their own usual stupidity, forgetfulness, depression, irritated spite, and sheer incapacity: as when you look at a certain kind of problem in a field for which you have no talent, and nothing happens, the quick insight does not flow.

Why should not the whole human race be given the capacity to experience and use that intensely individual genius which we reverence in just a few? Let us not comfort ourselves in our present condition by false and vulgar prejudices: that genius is necessarily unhappy, that geniuses are all the same, that the greatly talented are necessarily unstable or lopsided in personality, that they lack the common touch, that they are impractical. These problems all people have, and if anything great genius is often remarkably free of them. The unhappiness of genius is less due to inherent flaws in the nature of genius itself than to the fact that, having learned to fly, the genius feels more exasperatingly the crippling handicaps that all human beings labor under, and to the "inhuman dearth of noble natures" about them, as Keats put it. Perhaps through biotechnical means we may be able eventually to free the choked genius of our species: and having done this we would already be on the way to angelic intelligence and love. Of course a caution is in order: the biotechnical tools will themselves take artistic genius of a high order to wield without oversimplifying the problems or their solutions: and to this point we must return.

But our future evolution may well proceed in a fashion which partially transcends the strictly biological altogether. Gradually we are learning to approximate the capacities of the human mind by means of cybernetic artificial intelligence. Can there be any doubt that an understanding of the working of Mind will follow our understanding of the working of life and that just as we are now able to synthesize living matter, so we will be able to synthesize self–conscious thought and feeling and imagination? One day that evil distinction between the artificial and the natural will be thrown down, and we will have escaped the mind–forged manacles which alienate us from the creative and self–reflective evolution of the rest of nature. On that day we will have extended our minds and spirits into dimension beyond dimension; we will have a direct neural–cybernetic interface with our thinking machines, and through them to all of nature; we will feel as stones and flames and petals feel, because the instruments by which we register their experience will be directly connected to our nervous systems. All nature will be our home and our body.

And of course it always was, as the Zen sages tell us. But it is a peculiar thing about us, that we can at best feel only briefly and distantly the things that we know ought to make this world, even at the worst of times, a very paradise in every moment. We can know the infinitely interesting miracle of being, but are most of the time somehow divided as by a curtain from the actuality of it as experience. Why should not nature simply be waiting for us, with our great natural technical intelligence, to simply plug ourselves in to the universe?—to complete a new loop of feedback in the world? Perhaps our unhappiness, our frustrated rage, our cruel despair, comes from the unconscious realization that though it is what we were built for, we haven't gotten around to it yet. Nature cannot do it by herself, and thus evolved us, a special quintessence of the soul of nature, her "dearest–selved spark" as Hopkins says in *That Nature is a Heraclitean Fire and of the comfort of the Resurrection*, to do it for her. Perhaps the happiness of scientists and artists and saints is that they come closest to this in–feeling and participation, though by means which are only traditional and are as yet truncated of the new sensorium that needs to be added.

But the traditional means are indeed pretty wonderful in themselves. Indeed, it will be a part of the new science to recognize just how subtle and marvelous they are. The arts are already an empirical craft of artificial intelligence, a means of creating programs in paint, sound, stone, action or words that embody their makers' angelic insight yet survive their makers to be reincarnated when booted into the brain circuitry of other people. The traditional arts are also a way of getting access to the enormous integrating powers, the tact and instinct of nature at her best, that lie dormant in the human brain. Thus they are an essential partner with the new science and technology in creating and begetting those future beings that we see in our visions of angels. By itself the new technique would be shallow, a technical fix with possibly disastrous consequences: monsters or chilly abortions. Only when the sensibility of a Mozart, a Shakespeare, a Velásquez, a Murasaki, a Louis Armstrong is added to that of a Von Neumann or a Francis Crick, will the miracle have a chance of happening. And the artists themselves are special partly because they in turn have more immediate access to the angels they are helping to bring to birth. We can perhaps agree that if this work is not impossible, it might be a project as worthy as the building of the cathedrals and the construction of classical Greek civilization—something to replace the anomie of our century with a commitment that the whole world can share.

There is a curious circularity in the last paragraph that will bring us to the last point in this odd exploratory essay. Let us digress for a moment. Recently brain science has been revolutionized by the new concept of "top–down" causality (Roger Sperry's term). Brain science still concedes that the components of the brain—its atoms, molecules, cells, and anatomy—indeed partially determine, in a "bottom–up" fashion, what happens on the holistic level of thoughts, decisions, and feelings. But it is becoming increasingly clear that there exists a very powerful top–down causality, wherein we can change the chemistry and electrical activity of our brains by means of our choices, actions, knowledge, acquired habits, creative efforts and willed attitudes: the whole governing the parts.

But if the lower hierarchical levels of the brain are both causing and being caused by the higher levels, then the brain's activity is an essentially circular—or, better, a spiral or helical—process. It is a feedback system determining itself and determining its own process of self–determining. Now if the brain is an elegant microcosm of the universe—and it would be hard to see how we could have survived as a species if it were not, for otherwise it would always be wrong about the world and thus have led us into extinction—then the universe itself must be such a part–whole, top–down–bottomup feedback system too.

But it is also clear that the wholeness of the universe is an emergent property. As more and more sensitive organisms evolve to observe it, escaping the relative solipsism of the subatomic and atomic levels of being, so the universe assumes more and more a coherent unity. On a starry night we can see, in a sketchy and synoptic way, nearly half of it: but it takes specially and recently evolved eyes and brains to do so. If the holistic level of the universe is still only emerging, then we must identify the past with part–to–whole, bottom–up causality and the future with whole–to–part, top–down causality. That is, if the universe is something like a brain, the brain–parts of the universe are its past, and its mind is its future. We might even define the past and future, and thus time itself, by means of such a distinction.

But if the process of determining, of causality, goes both ways in time—bottom–up in the futurewards direction, top–down in the pastwards direction—then the universe itself is just such an iterative, spiral feedback system as is the brain. It is not just a linear process, and we must abandon all merely linear models of time. As a nonlinear system the universe is one of a class of systems now being investigated by chaos theory, fractal mathematics, and the theory of nonlinear, dissipative, self–organizing dynamical processes. Every event and object in the world has in a sense been round and round the great circuit of material and final cause an infinite number of times: its origins determining its present state, its results determining its origins. Thus every event in the world is infinitely rich; there is indeed infinity in a grain of sand, eternity in a flower. And this infinity, this eternity is not the vacuous and otiose thing that we find in classical metaphysics and set theory, but an active, open–ended, transformative infinity, a generativeness, like Chomskyan grammar. Every experience we have, if we were to see it properly, is infinitely deep, fully involving the creative and voluntary energy of the universe as a whole.

Here of course we are on the frontiers of theology: and before that prospect, the speculative tongue turns almost to stone. But there is one step between us and that blinding light, one further mediation or ratio of speculative understanding: the angels. And even if they do not exist, is not the very thought of them an active warrant of their reality as causes?—for are not thoughts causes?

ANGELS AND IMAGINATION

THE DETHRONEMENT OF THE ANGELS

LOUISE COWAN

Several striking images in Dante's *Paradiso* provide insight into the relation of angels to humanity and hence into the structure of the spiritual universe. One such image is of a point of immaterial light, so bright in its effulgence that "the eye on which it blazes needs must close because of its great keenness"[1] (XXVIII, 17–18). Beatrice informs Dante that the heavens and all nature hang from this point and that the descending circles he observes are angelic choirs.

She names and explains the nine orders of angels, adhering to the generally accepted structure of three triads first advanced by Dionysius the Areopagite in his *Celestial Hierarchy*: Seraphim, Cherubim, Thrones; Dominions, Virtues, Powers; Principalities, Archangels, Angels. All have their degree of blessedness according to the depth to which their sight penetrates the sacred truth "in which every intellect finds rest." These spiritual beings were created, she says,

> Not for gain of good unto Himself, which cannot be, but that
> His splendor might, in resplendence, say, "*Subsisto*"—in His
> eternity beyond time, beyond every other bound, as it pleased
> Him, the eternal Love opened into new loves. (XXIX, 13–18)

The angels are so numerous that there is no mortal language or concept to express their great abundance. Nor is there any limit to their variety: "The Primal Light that irradiates them all is received by them in as many ways as are the splendors to which It joins Itself" (XXIX, 136–38). Beatrice notes with pleasure Dante's "high desire" to know more of such heavenly matters and warns him that the images he has been seeing, beautiful as they are, are but "the shadowy prefaces of their truth" (XXX, 78). And indeed Dante's vision is clarified as he moves on to higher and higher levels of imagination. At one point he sees flowers that appear to be permeated by burning sparks: "so into greater festival the flowers and the sparks did change before me that I saw both the courts of Heaven made manifest" (XXX, 94–96). "Both the courts of heaven": at last Dante sees, in addition to the angelic host, the mystical eternal rose that Beatrice calls "our city." This is the company of saints—those mortal beings who have lived and died in God's grace:

> In form then of a pure white rose the saintly host [the commu-nion of saints] was shown to me, which with His own blood Christ made His bride. But the other host [the choir of angels]—who, as it flies, sees and sings His glory who enamors it and the goodness which made it so great—like a swarm of bees which one moment enflower themselves and the next return where their work acquires savor—was descending into the great flower which is adorned with so many petals, and then reascending to where its love abides forever. They had their faces all of living flame, and their wings of gold, and the rest so white that no snow reaches such a limit. When they descended into the flower, from rank to rank they proffered of the peace and the ardor which they had acquired as they fanned their sides. (XXX, 1–18)

Even apart from its visual beauty, the image is striking. The two joyous, adoring heavenly bodies are separate, though joined in a single action. One is forever immaterial—pure spirit (the angels); the other is forever material (the saints)—composed of highly *rarefied* materiality, to be sure, of spiritual body, but body nonetheless. The angelic host, like a swarm of bees, surrounds the great rose, dipping into it and emerging, "reascend-ing to where its love abides forever," as bees return to the hive, and then again descending in a perpetual figure of praise and celebration. What does this image convey? For one thing, it attests that human flesh and blood will never become angelic, even in its highest form; that the angels are not the central actors in the drama, but mediators, ornamenters, enhancers, joyous expressers of the love and beauty of creation, their function adoration.

Dante is here giving visual form to the Church Fathers' view of the relation of angels to mankind, a tradition solidly established over centuries of developing doctrine. In his masterful *The Angels and their Mission*, Jean Daniélou speaks of "the joy of the angelic creation in seeing Christ lead humanity back into heaven at the Ascension" (48). He cites St. John Chrysostom's sermon on the Ascension, in which the great theologian points out that in this event (the ascension of Christ into heaven), "the angels have obtained what they were always waiting for": human nature raised to its beauty and glory. "Even though it has the honor of being exalted above them, they rejoice at our good, just as they suffered when we were deprived of it" (44–45). Chrysostom continues, "The angels and the martyrs meet today." One has only to look with eyes of faith to see them, he declares. "And if the Church is filled with angels, how much more is that true today when their Lord has risen into heaven! The whole air about us is filled with angels" (67). Dante's poem is imbued with this vision of the plenitude of angels, rejoicing at the beauty of redeemed humanity. Thus this greatest of medieval poets, with his intensely personal interiorization of a psychic journey, is able to work within a meticulously articulated theological structure in a quite different manner from Byzantine artists and medieval painters, to make of highly specified images master figures of his own imagination.

In the very last lines of the poem Dante's "transhumanized" imagination (which, as he has told us, has aimed at something never before attempted in poetry) gives him another image of the spiritual reality which he is privileged to glimpse: he sees three great circles of light, within them a smaller circle. He struggles to see how the smaller circle is attuned to the larger—how man is contained in the godhead and yet not obliterated by it:

> Within the profound and shining subsistence of the lofty Light
> appeared to me three circles of three colors and one magnitude;

and one seemed reflected by the other, as rainbow by rainbow, and the third seemed fire breathed forth equally from the one and the other. . . . That circling which, thus begotten, appeared in Thee as reflected light, when my eyes had dwelt on it for a time, seemed to me depicted with our image within itself and in its own color, wherefore my sight was entirely set upon it. (XXX, 115–32)

The human person, then, the creature less spiritual than the angels, is the *imago dei*, the image of God, destined, for all his imperfections, to incorporation into the godhead. The angels, like the material universe, are in the realm of creatures outside this drama. For just as the physical world is not God, will never, like humanity, be ultimately drawn up into God, but will praise and celebrate him, so will the angels remain separate. Their task in eternity no longer will be that which they serve in time: of being helpers to a wounded humanity, guides and guardians of a damaged world—but of singing the glory of a fully realized form—a "new heaven and new earth." They remain the context for the drama, not the actors in it.

More than three centuries later, in the strange composite epic *Paradise Lost*, Milton is concerned likewise with making clear the difference between angelic and human natures.[2] Incorporating into his poem the teachings of Dionysius the Areopagite and the Church Fathers, particularly Augustine and Origen, as well as the Rabbinical writings, the Zohar and the Cabala, Milton was able to elaborate upon the two dissimilar destinies—the human and angelic.

In the famous Scale of Nature passage (Book V), the angel Raphael, having come to warn Adam of a diabolic visitor to the Garden, outlines the plan of God the Father in his creation of man. He begins, "O Adam, one Almighty is/ From whom all things flow and up to Him return. . . ." (V, 469–70). Things nearer to God are more spiritual, Raphael tells Adam, explaining the "Scale of Nature," or, as it was called by most thinkers until well after the Renaissance, the "Great Chain of Being." Body may gradually work itself up to spirit, Raphael informs his eager listener:

> . . . time may come when men
> With angels may participate. . . .
> . . . .
> Your bodies may at last turn all to spirit,
> Improved by tract of time, and winged ascend
> Ethereal, as we, or may at choice
> Here or in heav'nly paradises dwell. . . .
> (V, 493–500)

We may assume that Raphael is here detailing the *original* plan for the human race. The human person (made up of both Adam and Eve) is placed in an abundant and benevolent earthly situation, with a destiny of becoming increasingly spiritual, so that humanity may at last "turn all to spirit" and take its place with the angels, dwelling either on earth or in heaven. To make all this spiritual progress, human beings need only to follow their supreme gift, Right Reason, an inner light which can rule over bodily elements in the human composition.

In the Genesis myth, according to Karol Wotyla, Adam and Eve have an "original unity"; together they make up the human person (God created man—"male and female created he them"). Milton follows this Biblical tradition in making the two together the "hero" in that most fearful of epic tasks, the founding of an entire race of mortals—Adam representing the intellectual and spiritual portion of the human person, Eve the sensuous and passionate. She is the daring, bold, creative element in this unity that constitutes the *imago dei.*

In the scene where, knowing of Satan's invasion of the garden, Raphael counsels Adam concerning the importance of relying on reason rather than feeling, the angel is troubled by Adam's over–fondness for Eve. The memory of her creation is vivid and intense; Adam speaks of his "transported touch":

> here passion first I felt
> Commotion strange. . . .
> . . . [and now] when I approach

> Her loveliness, so absolute she seems
> And in herself complete, . . .
> . . . that what she wills to do or say
> Seems wisest, virtuousest, discreetest, best;
> All higher knowledge in her presence falls
> Degraded. . . .

He suggests that perhaps Nature failed in him and left some part

> Not proof enough such object to sustain
> Or from my side subducting, took perhaps
> More than enough; at least on her bestowed
> Too much of ornament. . . .

The angel then "with contracted brow" rebukes Adam, advising him not to accuse nature. Adam has been given right reason, his majestic instructor informs him, which should act as safeguard against temptations from lower powers. "What is it that so fascinates you?" Raphael asks Adam. "An outside? Is the sense of touch, which was also given to animals, so precious?" The angel is alarmed and indignant: "Be careful," he says, "that you do not overrate your sensual appetites."

But Adam's destiny is already settled. Eve is his other half; she is his orientation with the reality of the world, the mystery of matter. Adam's fall is directly related to this hidden knowledge which not even the angels possess. He knows he is one with Eve; at her creation he uttered the joyous cry, "Bone of my bone, flesh of my flesh." It is this choice of his own identity that makes the fall of Adam, seen allegorically and in retrospect, virtually inevitable.

If Adam's mode of knowledge, like the angel's, is predominantly spiritual—an inner contemplation and an inner structuralizing (higher and lower reason)—then Eve's is the kind of knowledge that angels by their very nature cannot have and that Adam possesses to a lesser degree than Eve, believing it to be "lower" than reason. Hers is preeminently the knowledge of touch: of material things uniting with material things: light waves caressing and entering the cornea and coming to rest, tenderly, on the optic nerve; of small, rarefied particles of matter taken into the body through the nostrils and impressing themselves on the olfactory nerve; of objects themselves in their full bodiness being taken into the mouth, chewed and savored, swallowed, and assimilated. The relationship between humanity and things could hardly be more intimate: inscape becomes instress—a knowledge that cannot be known outside, or above, the body. Eve, then, is declaring herself for perception, for feeling, for direct relation to things through the senses. What this capacity requires is a communion with the tangible world, a realization and appreciation of matter in the unique way of which the human is capable. Adam and the angel think alike, for the most part; they both think rationally, governed by right reason and intuition, a sense of the truth of structures. Eve merges with things, feels with and through them in a giving and taking, an I–Thou relationship that is guided by other laws than those that govern the reasoning process—by an ontology of spiritual pattern imprinted on the physical world. Hers is essentially a sacramental mode of knowledge which, before the Fall, is whole and immediate.

After the fruit from the Tree of Knowledge has been eaten in a kind of declaration of self, imagination has been set in motion, and both the creature *man* and the creation *world* are changed. Adam has already been affected, and it would be false of him not to recognize this actuality. Not only the Genesis story but also the New Testament testifies to the indissoluble unity of man and woman: the two are spoken of by Christ as "one flesh"; and, as St. Paul makes clear, the husband's body belongs to his wife, whom he must then love as he loves his own body. With the fall of the innocent sensual way of knowing, human thought and reason are likewise tainted. Adam is merely acknowledging what has already been accomplished when he takes the fruit from Eve and, without argument, devours it.

The consequent corruption of all things physical spoils the original plan; Milton speaks of man's now having to proceed as from "a second stock." That stock from which the new tree will grow is the second person of the Trinity, who empties himself of his divinity to become man and take on the mysterious knowledge of the flesh as he assumes the penalty for human sin. As Ladislaus Boros has written (in *Angels and Men*), "The old order was replaced by a new one. Jesus' arrival was the coming of a new order, in which [he] superseded intermediary powers. They lost their faculty of government forever" (32). Boros cites Paul for the main text supporting this interpretation: "On that cross he discarded the cosmic powers and authorities like a garment; he made a public spectacle of them and led them as captives in his triumphal procession" (Col 2:15).

The cosmic powers Jesus discarded were the structures of the original creation, in which the angels (both fallen and unfallen) were direct governors of those things above man, at times as "flaming ministers," judges, and adversaries. They controlled the universe with rigid laws to which man was subject. According to St. Paul:

> During our minority we were slaves to the elemental spirits of the universe.... Formerly when you did not acknowledge God, you were the slaves of beings which in their nature are no gods. But now that you do acknowledge God—or rather, now that he has acknowledged you—how can you turn back to the ... spirits of the elements? Why do you propose to enter their service all over again? (Gal 4:3–9)

and further: God set Jesus "far above all government and authority, all power and dominion, and any title of sovereignty that can be named, not only in this age but in the age to come. He put everything in subjection beneath his feet. ..." (Eph 1:21–22). As Boros interprets it, what these Pauline texts are really describing is the dethronement of the angels—the good angels as well as the bad. The necessity for a redeemer cancelled the old world order and set into motion the new.

What caused this revolution in the divine plan was the fall of man, not the fall of the angels. Of the two, the dereliction of the rebel angels stemmed from an infinitely greater degree of malice. It consisted of knowingly choosing themselves rather than the love that animates the universe—of cutting off a portion of that "deep and dazzling darkness" at the center of God's creation, to use the words of the mystic Henry Vaughan. This act of absolute rebellion created an outer darkness where the creature rather than the creator can reign supreme. But it is an anomaly for the angels to be for themselves, they who exist as the highest reverberation of creation, who, though they have as their purpose its guidance, could not exist without the lowest foundation of materiality. They are, one might say, the spiritual extensions of that materiality—the invisible structures of the visible. Hence their rebellion creates a kind of vacuum and an anti–center at the heart of things, a howling abyss of "weeping and wailing and gnashing of teeth." And because their action was taken in absolute knowledge, they cannot repent and change. Nor can God because of them change his plan for the ultimate outcome of his creation.

Man, the crown of creation, given lordship over the animals, dominion over the earth, may be more easily forgiven for desiring not so much independence from God as union with the creation that God himself called "good," the preference of the gift over the Giver, as the seventeenth–century poet George Herbert wrote. But man's rebellion (his fall into guilty knowledge, inordinate desire, suffering, responsibility, and penance) precipitated nature's fall along with his own. And the altered position of man and the created universe affected as well the position of the angels. The fall of some from their own ranks did not modify the general role of the angels; but the fall of man changed forever the structures of heaven. The coming of Christ as redeemer of guilty man "dethroned the angels," took away their governing powers, though it did not change their nature—did not in fact lessen their spiritual force, which they still exert for the good of man and for God's glory. The Church Fathers speak of the angels as "guardians," "protectors," "superintendents," "overseers," "shepherds," "herdsmen." Daniélou quotes Eusebius in a passage where he brings together all the names of the angels: "Fearing lest sinful mankind should be without government and without guidance, like herds of cattle, God gave them protectors and superintendents, the holy angels, in the forms of captains and shepherds. His First–born Son is set above all of these" (70).

But, as Boros acknowledges, the angels remain magnificent and terrible presences, "far above everything human." Full of majesty, "they are the light and ardour of creation, and the essence of all feeling and emotion." He refers to Pauline theology, where they are called "principles of the world," indicating that the reality of things stems from them. Angels are present in our daily circumstances and in historical events. "They are present to us everywhere and incessantly, in the full immediacy of being. Hence our world is holy and the inner space of creation is already paradise" (35).

In the far reaches of our minds, we dimly remember the original plan. We sense the angelic presences and aspire to them. Our bodies partake not only of materiality, however, but, according to the Scriptural account, of fallen materiality; and our minds are subject as well to inclinations from the fallen angels. But the second plan for man and creation posits less a law of obedience than an adoption into freedom. In the second dispensation, the true path of virtue for the creature formed "a little lower than the angels" is imagination and love. Both of these actions, in proceeding through suffering and labor, continue, with the help of the angels, that process of *poiesis*, unique to humankind, that gradually transforms the earth.

THE ANGELIC IMAGINATION: ASPIRATION AND DEGRADATION

DONA S. GOWER

Jacques Maritain, in his study *The Dream of Descartes*, ascribes to the famous French philosopher the impetus which served to spread like a disease a disorder which has, in literature at least, characterized the modern psyche. Maritain comments:

> Cartesian dualism breaks man up into two complete substances, joined to one another none knows how: on the one hand, the body which is only geometrical extension; on the other, the soul which is only thought—an angel inhabiting a machine and directing it by means of the pineal gland.

> . . . for human intellection is living and fresh only when it is centered upon the vigilance of sense perception. The natural roots of our knowledge being cut, a general drying up in philosophy and culture resulted, a drought for which romantic tears were later to provide only an insufficient remedy. . . . Affectivity will have its revenge.[1]

Acknowledging his debt to Maritain, Allen Tate developed the notion of the angelic imagination in his famous essay on that subject, the subtitle of which is "Poe as God." Tate argued that Poe intuited the harmful consequences of that gross dissociation between feeling, will, and intellect that often forms the basis for his fiction and poetry.

Yet Poe, like his characters, according to Tate, also suffered from the same disorder: a "hypertrophy" of those faculties, each in disharmonious and destructive activity and oblivious to the "natural roots of our knowledge" in the corporeal world. Insisting on analogy as a mode of knowledge which encompasses imagination, cognition, and reason, Tate concludes that those who would "circumvent the natural world" and, like Poe, stand "in the place of God" as creator of a subjective, quasi–divine cosmos, are vulnerable to annihilation from sheer "exhaustion"—what Tate calls "the exhaustion of force as a consequence of . . . intellectual liberation from the sensible world."[2] He summarizes his argument thus:

> The reach of our imaginative enlargement is perhaps no longer than the ladder of analogy, at the top of which we may see all, if we still wish to see anything, that we have brought up with us from the bottom, where lies the sensible world. If we take nothing with us to the top but our emptied, angelic intellects, we shall see nothing when we get there. Poe as God sits silent in darkness. Here the movement of tragedy is reversed: there is no action. Man as angel becomes a demon who cannot initiate the first motion of love, and we can feel only compassion with his suffering, for it is potentially ours.[3]

Man's envy of the angelic capacity to know essences directly, instead of seeing "as through a glass, darkly," has influenced the whole history of our race, not simply the nineteenth and twentieth centuries. And Tate is right to emphasize that these tail–ends of the modern world which began in the Renaissance particularly dramatize the wide–spread effects of the desire for a plane of existence which is unencumbered by the limitations of the senses as well as by the exigencies of external reality.

That which masquerades as noble aspiration for a pure state of being is, in reality, an attempt to assert the self as absolute. By rejecting analogy as the primary mode of human knowledge—a knowledge dependent upon the senses and on the corporeal world—the seeker would emulate the angels without the benefit of the immediate possession of the Beatific Vision. Instead, the mirror of one's own pure intellect becomes a universe of its own which must guard always against the intrusion of anything that might contradict the purity of that image.

Such a condition of soul instigates a war—a war with creation, materiality, as well as with God. In the dark recesses of the Judeo–Christian myth of the Fall is the power of angels gone awry. Milton's treatment in *Paradise Lost* of the war in heaven suggests the kind of sin to which the angelic intellect is liable.[4] For, as Milton shows us in Lucifer's response to Abdiel, the closer the essence to its source, the more likely it is to mistake its own reflection for the shining:

> . . . Remember'st thou
> Thy making, while the Maker gave thee being?
> We know no time when we were not as now;
> Know none before us, self–begot, self–raised
> By our own quick'ning power . . .
> Our puissance is our own. . . . (857–864)

As Satan, Lucifer embodies the lesson Tate posits for man: the "angel becomes a demon who cannot initiate the first motion of love." And his sin is a kind of subjectivity that cannot accept the grandeur of the angelic self as analogous to a higher being. He must be the author of his own creation and, as such, "cannot initiate the first motion of love." Therefore, he must seek to annihilate rather than to create.

Eve, only a little lower than the angels herself, is tempted like Lucifer to take on divinity; yet Milton is kinder to the first parents than he is to the angels who fell. Eve's love for Adam moves her out of her own egotistical concerns and, ultimately, to embrace the now–fallen world's body in all its imperfections. The primal parents, Milton shows us, are willing to live with the consequences of an intellectual sin that permanently wounded nature itself. And their love foreshadows the incarnate love that would redeem both them and the world, the love taking upon itself the full measure of corporeal existence and with it the imperfection and all the consequences of that original sin which stemmed from a spurious aspiration to "be like god."

The repetition of the angelic sin in human beings, of course, can be seen in plays like Marlowe's *Dr. Faustus* and in countless other dramas of the sixteenth and early seventeenth centuries. Faustus wishes to know by direct revelation the secrets of creation, rather than by going through the dark glass of the visible but God–made world. Faustus' sin is that rejection of analogy characteristic of men who would be angels. Shakespeare's Iago, however, in his "motiveless malevolence," as Coleridge called it, must destroy the good simply because it exists in contradistinction to his own ego. He represents one of few examples in literature—and, I suspect, in life—of that genuinely Luciferian iniquity that curses the good for its own sake. Iago becomes the enemy of all substance, for to be absolute himself he must destroy anything outside his own spiritual circumference.

Milton's epic, composed in the mid–seventeenth century, at the end of the Puritan experiment to set up God's kingdom on earth, another act of hybris worthy of the angelic imagination, sums up the cultural crisis that has haunted us since. In the scientism and deism of the eighteenth century, "know then thyself, presume not God to scan / The proper study of mankind is man," we have another subjective and angelic posture that has proved no less destructive than the dark supernaturalism the Puritans feared even as they burned witches. The eighteenth century, with its notion of progress and the infinite perfectibility of man, worshipped its own angelic image, thereby excluding analogy, and projected its geometric shape on science and gardens and art alike, nearly always failing in the very originality it sought.

As Maritain pointed out in the essay on Descartes, the "general drying up in philosophy and culture" would need more than "romantic tears" to alleviate it. Yet Georg Lukacs in *Theory of the Novel* emphasizes the artist's awareness of the drying up that occurs when human beings attempt the kind of purity that we associate with the angelic sphere. Tate and Maritain knew Lukacs, and I rather suspect that his notion of the demons that characterize modernity influenced their own development of the idea of the angelic imagination. Lukacs claims that two demons have possessed the modern psyche: the demon of abstract idealism and the demon of the romanticism of disillusionment. Operating on the premise that "the epic and the novel, these two major forms of great epic literature, differ from one another not by their authors' fundamental intentions but by the given historico–philosophical realities with which the authors were confronted." Lukacs continues, "The novel is the epic of an age in which the extensive totality of life is no longer directly given, in which the immanence of meaning in life has become a problem, yet which still thinks in terms of totality."[5] Abstract idealism, a fundamental form of angelism, Lukacs says is a "narrowing of the soul":

> It is the mentality which chooses the direct, straight path towards the realization of the ideal; which, dazzled by the demon, forgets the existence of any distance between the ideal and the idea, between psyche and soul; which, with the most authentic and unshakable faith, concludes that the idea, because it should be, necessarily must be, and, because reality does not satisfy this *a priori* demand, thinks that reality is bewitched by evil demons and that the spell can be broken and reality can be redeemed either by finding a magic password or by courageously fighting the evil forces.[6]

Lukacs understands that the demon of abstract idealism is the sire of the second demon:

> The romanticism of disillusionment not only followed abstract idealism in time and history, it was also conceptually its heir, the next historico–philosophical step in *a priori* utopianism. . . . In Romanticism . . . the self, cut off from transcendence, recog- nizes itself as the source of the ideal reality, and, as a necessary consequence as the only material worthy of self–realization.[7]

Any number of examples in modern literature can be cited. Ahab, in Melville's *Moby Dick*, represents the angel/demon of the first sort, and Angel Clare, in Thomas Hardy's *Tess of the D'Urbervilles*, embodies the second. The first, incapable of accepting the paradoxical quality of the very texture of life in a fallen world, sets forth to destroy evil but becomes the adversary of the God who permitted it. The second, spinning the world from his own imagination, annihilates Tess by telling her, after her confession of impurity, that she is not the woman he loved: "I repeat, you are not the same woman."

Only by reclaiming that totality of existence to which Lukacs refers can a culture hope to ameliorate the drought. That totality mandates a return to analogy as a mode of knowledge, for only by that embodiment of spirit in matter, fallen and imperfect corporeality, can a people hope to engender a new age in which the human psyche can function in its proper sphere—the world's body.

Richard Wilbur, one of our finest living poets, has articulated the primary condition for humankind's "initiation of the first motion in love." In *Love Calls Us to the Things of This World*, Wilbur explores humankind's flirtation with the angelic imagination and provides a paradigm for the human mode of analogy.[8] Paradoxically enough, Wilbur's poem seems to suggest, when "Love calls us to the things of this world," we are most likely to see the angels themselves and to perceive their function as intermediaries between us and the objects of our thought.

The poem begins with the awakening of the soul before it has descended into the body after a night's sleep—an allusion to the Indian belief that the soul departs the body during sleep, an imitation of death. The soul, the speaker says, "hangs for a moment bodiless and simple / as false dawn." Wilbur prepares the reader for the spurious experience of angelism by such phrases as "false dawn," something beautiful but deceptive. Mistaking yards of laundry hanging on pulleys outside the window for pure spirits, the soul believes the "air is all awash with angels." Indeed, what the soul sees are disembodied clothes moved not by angelic wearers but by the wind. Yet the illusion is powerful:

> Some are in bed–sheets, some are in blouses,
> Some are in smocks: but truly there they are.
> Now they are rising together in calm swells

Of halcyon feeling, filling whatever they wear
With the deep joy of their impersonal
breathing.

Just as the human soul is momentarily liberated from the body in sleep, the fluttering clothes seem free from the limitations of the flesh and able to soar or "swoon down into so rapt a quiet / That nobody seems to be there." Of course, no body is what the soul most desires, for a descent to the physical circumscribes boundaries for the spirit and forces it to know through objects, through analogy, the power of incarnate love.

At first the soul resists "all that it is about to remember, / From the punctual rape of every blessed day," the return to the body and to the "things of this world." Although crying "Oh, let there be nothing on earth but laundry, / Nothing but rosy hands in the rising steam / And clear dances done in the sight of heaven," the waking soul does not ultimately reject its proper habitation in the corporeal sphere that is proper to humanity. Wilbur juxtaposes the pure light of the sun, analogous to divine love, with the action of the soul as it embraces the body:

> Yet, as the sun acknowledges
> With a warm look the world's hunks and colors,
> The soul descends once more in bitter love
> To accept the waking body, saying now
> In a changed voice as the man yawns and rises,
> "Bring them down from their ruddy gallows;
> Let there be clean linen for the backs of thieves;
> Let lovers go fresh and sweet to be undone.
> And the heaviest nuns walk in a pure floating
> Of dark habits,
> > keeping their difficult balance."

The analogic imagination that is specifically human but informed by the principle of incarnation—that which marries the visible and invisible realms—triumphs in Wilbur's poem. The descent in "bitter love" to the

---

"waking body" brings the wholeness suggested by the reciprocity of being in the "waking" of both body and soul as the "man," cognizant of the "delicate balance" of matter and spirit in a fallen but grace–infused world.

"The world is awash with angels." But, as Tom Moore has said, they usually contact us. They seldom appear at our calling, though they are willing to be our messengers as well as the messengers of God. When we see the "splendour in the grass, the glory in the flower," an angel has been the intermediary in that poetic process which Maritain calls the "interpenetration between man and things." Those moments of creative intuition come to us by analogy, when we are most vulnerable to something outside ourselves which incarnates, like God–made–man, the essence of the divine act of love. Just as Angels are grateful to descend to this priceless realm, their sparks fly upward, as Louise Cowan has said, after they embrace the rose of this world, flapping their wings in a shared eros for that sensual manifestation of divine love.

Angels: A Way of Working, of Being Worked on (Worked Over)

Robert Trammell

> Every angel is terrifying.
> —Rilke

> We must get out of the bad habit of seeing Angels and Archangels as fairy-like winged creatures entirely for the good of mankind. They are units of specialized energy. Angels are more like guided missiles than bodiless babies with wings.
> —William Gray, *Quabalah Renovata*

> To put a story or explanation on an image is like putting a biography on an angel. It makes the angel an alternator. No lightning. It is like Christianity lightening the angels by whitening them iconically. They are dark. Ask Jacob or consult the angels of Rilke, or Hölderlin's angels of the house and year or Steven's necessary angel. The poets know. Angels are Hell, like images. They are to be wrestled. . . . Angels are messengers. But since they have no biographies, they bring no messages. They are the message.
> —David Miller, "Images, Angels, Bacon"

As 1988 was winding down and as this conference on/of Angels drew closer I was struggling with a way to approach it/them or even better to have them approach me. I wanted to see one or some but could not. I talked to people in bars, at parties, at work, anywhere/everywhere and was swamped, deluged. Angels all over the place/lots of stories. Everybody seemed to have seen Angels but me. Not felt them but seen them. Marilyn said she saw them all the time, all over the country. Whole flocks, clouds of Angels around her bed. Kris said they were on her bedroom wall and had been there all her life. But nobody seemed to have seen any in the kitchen or the bathroom. Usually in the bedroom. I'm not sure if they show up at Angel Conferences. & lots of Guardian Angels. All personal, kind of furry, white friends. Then someone told me I was an Angel which really confused me. Could I be one and not know it? Somebody else said they saw my Angel hovering about me. None of this worked. I was happy for everybody and all their Angels but still wanted one of my own. Not even that Jung/Corbin/Olson notion worked. As Olson puts it that "the soul, / in its progressive rise"

> . . . —it sends out
> on the path ahead the Angel
> it will meet. . . .[1]

& now I'm working, being worked on. Maybe what matters more anyway is that they "see" me than I them. I don't think you can quite trust anyone who says they are an Angel. It could just be an Angel Mask they got on. The good ones are the ones to be most wary of. They are usually just distractions.

I want a big ol' giant hundred foot tall red Gabriel like Muhammad saw, but will probably wind up again with "An Angel Flying Too Close To The Ground." Just as the baby was about to roll over the curb and be swept down the storm sewer an Angel appeared in the gutter, knelt and caught, cradled the infant. In a dream The Angel of Death was strangling me but he got called away to a more important death and I woke up in a Bergman movie. In Ballagredean, the West of Ireland, I was drunk and wet. It was about 25°F at night and I threw my sleeping bag over the fence into a pool of water. Soaked it good and had to sleep in it. Could have frozen to death but an Angel appeared and took me to a warm place for the night. I woke with a Magpie on my chest. I was rested and warm. &

Bobby Blue Bland sings: "Falling in love with you Angel is like falling in love with a dream." In darkness, chaos I wrestle One to the ground. but she's no Angel she's just got wings. In the dark within like Coleridge's Devil was an Angel of Light who chose the Dark within.[2] So many of them want to appear to Blake that they got to make appointments. Getting tired, confused and I haven't seen an Angel yet. Serpents in India are an order of Angels. & I'm at that point where Yeats says "The only legitimate passivity is that which follows exhaustion of the intellect. Then guidance comes."[3] He saw it as a struggle in which all his faculties had to be used to grasp, receive, & wrestle with the visiting Angel of Inspiration. In the Breath? In the Word? Are they the dark matter that makes up 90% of the cosmos that science knows nothing about or perhaps some kind of conditional elementarities who the smaller they are the stronger they become.

In the meantime the more I tried to concentrate on Angels the more snakes appeared. I had a rattlesnake skin that Roxy Gordon had given me and some old wooden cigar boxes that I had started making little tableaux with snakes, birds and eggs in. & God knows making Art beats thinking any day. I kept making them & the snakes were becoming wilder, redder, fierier. Then it was Christmas which I spent in New Jersey drinking Jack Daniels and watching my sister's huge television. After a couple of weeks of New Jersey, Jack Daniels, and television, I was ready again for Angels but only snakes were waiting. I made more boxes. It wasn't till I was reading a book that dealt with Coleridge and his Angels that I ran across something that made everything click into place. Seraphim are flying, fiery serpents. The Hebrew word S'R'PH could signify either a serpent or an angelic being. Then Wilkins translates from the Sanskrit: ". . . describing this luxuriant paradise of Eendra, so remarkable for being guarded by serpents breathing fire, the flaming seraphim of Scripture, for saraph means a serpent." & as Rabbi Bechai observes: "this is the mystery of our holy language that a serpent is called a saraph, as an angel is called seraph."[4] And I was someplace like in the bodhimandala of my soul. That place I'd read about in *The Vimalakirti Nirdesa Sutra*—"a circle, holy site or place of enlightenment; a place where a Bodhisattva"[5] or an Angel appears and you get a glimpse of it. & this One that appears is a hot one, on fire. The Hebrew root of seraphim being "to burn." These burn with Love. They are on fire and their sword burns and they are extremely dangerous. That fiery, flying serpent that Isaiah saw above the throne of God. The one who guards the gates of Paradise & the Way to The Tree of Life. One puts a hot coal to the lips of Isaiah. They are Hell. Satan was one. & they purify. Seraphim burn out spiritual impurities & they do it with Love. Their planet is Mars. They burn out of us accumulations of useless mental and spiritual rubbish. They purify, and if we have failed to correct our faults by other means they will not let us into Paradise without using their fiery swords on us. The only way we can prevent this is to let go, to become truly detached from all within ourselves that is spiritually useless.[6] Angelsnakes, plumed serpents like Quetzalcoatl. & after these angelsnakes have purified us the true spiritual waters are freed. These same waters are released in the Rig Veda when the hero Indra slays the dragon/snake with his Thunderbolt. As in Yahweh's victory over Leviathen & Zeus' over Typhon.

Now what interested me was how I got to this Angel or how this seraphim was getting to me. The more I tried to use my conscious, rational mind, the more I looked to Heaven, the further away, the further underground I drove the angel until there was no deeper to go and the winged serpent forced its way up and out, bursting like a rocket.

Pat Berry's "Stopping: A Mode of Animation" in which she deals with the Perseus/Medusa story as a way of working oneself out of Standstill had been important to me but this was the first time I had been able to watch the Myth unfold in my soul. You know, if you go head on at this monster you'll go blind, be torn limb from limb, get killed and burned to a cinder. So you got to come at it from an angle. Look at the problem's reflection or don't look at all just close your eyes and grope around in the dark. And if you can fumble around and find the monster—of course it helps to be invisible—and get its head chopped off, its head full of snakes, then Chrysor of the Golden Sword and Pegasus spring from the body and as the essay ends:

Wings: there are wings on Pegasus. He is wings within the body of a horse. . . . There are wings here beyond the bees and butterflies and little cherubic angels—wings that stomp and snort, that buck and gallop. So within nature's depths, its matter, we find a body of air; within stasis we find movement; in that awe-full image of stopping there is a rush of wings, an animal power in the insubstantial air.[7]

Now it's cooking. Frank Tolbert sends me a drawing of a snake to wish me a Happy Chinese New Year. The Year of the Snake. & wings. Another element is birds and wings. Snakes & birds, a deathly combination. I start to read Lawrence's *Plumed Serpent*, put it down and get my *Larousse Encyclopedia of Myth* instead and find in it a picture I'd never seen. Right in the front, the first picture there in full color, I stumble upon a picture of Perseus, Medusa and Pegasus. A little bas-relief (I think little, no dimensions are given) from the British Museum. It is a wonder and a revelation and stands everything on its head. Pegasus has no wings nor are there winged shoes on Perseus of Seriphos. The only one with wings and they are splendid ones, is Medusa. OK, so she's ugly, her body is Angelic. It's like she's saying: "Thanks Perseus. You can have that ugly head. Take it to Athena. I'm glad to be shut of it." & she opens her arms in gratitude. She spreads her wings. She is free to fly up, out, away from her cave now that Athene's wearing her snake head/mask for maximum protection. Now that Pallas Athene's got a new Gorgoneion to decorate her aegis. Athene whose father Pallas, according to one version, has winged feet and in variants is otherwise winged.[8]

& Now I feel stuck again, caught up in, not so much her story, but from looking, from looking at her cut-off head that Perseus rides away with. I am stuck in the middle of the myth. Could be I need to lose my head so I can get on with this. Have I burned here long enough now? I turn my eyes away to see with new eyes and the air fills with flaming serpents. Ready now for the next inner level of Existence.

In *The Ladder of Lights* about half way up the Quabalah Tree of Life at Sephirah 5, in Geburah where the Angel Order is Seraphim whose attributes are Strength, Severity, Fear. If we can get past the searing bite of the Seraphim's sword we move on to meet the Archangel Khamael in Briah. & guess what Khamael is. KHAB means to feel pain, to suffer, to sadden, and to make war. The name of this Archangel means "The Burner of God." Out of the frying pan and into The Burner of God. This is Satan's turf. Sammael, the Destroying Angel of Death, is linked with Khamael. As 1989 got under way, after I'd drunk enough firewater to get me thru the year, I was confronted with three archetypes with which I was going to have to deal. Two of them, angels and snakes, I've been talking about/working with up to this point, but the third was yet to be dealt with. It was Death, more specifically the Death of Tarot card #13. Now here in Sephirah 5 they all came together in Briah with The Burner of God and The Destroying Archangel of Death Khamael. This is a place of resistance. Geburah resists pure Divine Energy and makes possible conduction by Sephirah 6 Chesed. Khamael is called The Right Hand of God, the sword hand of God. Justice. Justice restores balance and harmony thruout the Tree.

Khamael sums up the activities of the Seraphim, and should be seen as a higher form of Mars, operating on spiritual levels. Nothing can pass further up the Tree unless purified by the power Khamael directs.

Looking at the Tree-Pattern here, we can appreciate the legend of the Sammael-Michael struggle, and the dualist concept of Jesus and Lucifer being twin souls, one saving and the other destroying the world. Chesed (Light/Mercy) and Geburah (Heat/Justice) in action. There is a tradition that when Lucifer, the most beautiful Archangel in Heaven fell, his beauty changed to the color of molten iron. In other words Light became Heat. Our planet changed from luminescent gas to an explosive fiery mass of matter, and life could not commence until its surface cooled sufficiently for the Light of the Sun to work its magic. Lucifer is imprisoned in the center of our planet as Heat, and still has enough power to blow it apart. Nevertheless if the heat at the earth's core cooled we should perish.

Khamael is governor of all that is associated with burning and so may be invoked to help us control our destructive tendencies beyond the necessity for their use.

They that emerge from Geburah . . . will be adepts of self-discipline and auto-correctors of unbalance. Health, harmony, and happiness becomes theirs of right because all causes of opposite conditions have been burned out by Geburic fires. It may seem strange that the way to Heaven lies thru Hell but it is a commonplace Pathway. Having encountered and survived Geburah, we should be in a state of mind to approach its balancing and complementary Sephirah Chesed which has to do with Mercy and Compassion.[9]

You got to get past these Guardians to enter Paradise.

And I am back in the Medusa story again. What flows from her head after it is hacked off? Winged, unbridled Pegasus, Chrysor of the Golden Sword and even tho we know little about Chrysor that Gold Sword resonates. And finally the blood flows out which Asclepius, the god of healing, collects. This blood has the power of Life and Death. And She spreads her wings. It is not the wings so much but She is related to Kali, her sister, who gives with her right hand while She holds a raised sword in her left. Who gives birth to all beings in the universe and whose long red tongue laps up their living blood. With her skull neckless and severed arms and legs decorate her. She is Black Time. Life and Death of all. Womb and Tomb. The primal, one-and-only, ultimate of nature, of whom the gods themselves are but functioning agents.

And as for Medusa, where did she get her wings? We know her head went on with Perseus back to Seriphos where he used it on the tyrant King Polydectes who had sent Perseus off to get the Gorgon's head but also to get rid of him, to get him out of the way so he, King Polydectes, could get, so he could have Perseus' mother Danae. But Perseus, to everyone's surprise, comes back with the head and aims it at the King and all of his retinue turning them all into stone as well as the rest of the isle of Seriphos which even today is full of rocks.

But what about her wings? In some versions of the myth both of her sister Gorgons have wings and she has none, in others they all three have them. This is before Perseus comes along. I go along with the first version cause after all She was the only mortal one of the three; the only one who could be killed, could be sacrificed. but She had a gift in her death for mankind. In her blood was the healing power of life and death. And when She becomes headless her gifts flow out in her blood and her wings grow gold and with arms open, wings spread She soars from her underworld cave. Call her what you will now. Snakeforce, Kundalini, Shakti, Angel, Medusa. She flies into consciousness from the fire chakra. Flying up from the belly into the head. Blasting the head off. This is the serpentine way of Perseus. Above this scene a Phoenix, an eagle fly. And all of it is about Angels and what needs to have attention paid to it. It is now a time for more Heat than Light. A Fire in the Darkness. Jung said that "If Angels are anything at all, they are personified transmitters of unconscious contents that are seeking expression."[10] I don't know that they are or need to be so much "personified" as that they are the thing itself, a way of working. The Work itself. They are the message. They surround me and wrap me in downy wings or they are suffocating me. The problem may be with the wings. the wings make it difficult to imagine them.

The Angel is the Opus.

These are fiery angel snakes devouring themselves. This is the alchemical solve et coagula, the double spiral. Shakti. The Angel from below. Tarot Card #14, the Devil. In Papus' *The Tarot of the Bohemians* there is a reproduction of an early Devil card with the alchemical word *solve* on one arm and *coagula* on the other.[11] Quicksilver/Mercury, the *solve* or dissolving agent, is the snake swallowing its own tail which is about to break free and to spin and spiral upwards with the red hot sulphur serpent. Burckhardt says:

> In the Hermetic tradition, Universal Nature in her latent condition is represented as a coiled up reptile. This is the Uroboros.

> Nature in her dynamic phase, on the other hand, is portrayed
> by means of the two serpents which in the form of the staff of
> Hermes, the caduceus, wind themselves around an axis.[12]

They are masculine Sulphur which is pure energy and a serpent without wings and feminine Quicksilver which is pure matter or a serpent with wings. They are Ida and Pingala that wind up thru the chakras. Hermes' staff works kinda like The Seraphim with the flaming sword guarding the door to Paradise. Hermes acquired his staff when one day he saw two snakes fighting. He struck them, tamed them and they wound themselves round his staff conferring on him the theurgic power of "binding" and "loosing." The means to turn chaos into cosmos, conflict into order, through the power of a spiritual act, which both discriminates and unites. Like Moses' rod that turns into a snake. (From *OED*: Theurgy—(1584) There is yet another art, which is called theurgie; wherein they work by good angels.) According to Jung, Mercury/Mercurius is "world-creating spirit concealed or imprisoned in matter," for which Uroboros, the tail-eating dragon, stands, the "oldest pictorial symbol in alchemy." For Mercurius "stands at the beginning and end of the work; he is the *prima materia*, the *nigredo*; as dragon he devours himself and as dragon he dies to rise again as the lapis."[13]

Angel work. Snake work. Mercurius complains that he is "sore tormented" with a fiery sword. Mercurius is the old serpent who already in paradise possessed "knowledge" since he was closely related to the Devil. It is the fiery sword brandished by the angel at the gates of Paradise that torments him and yet he himself is the sword.

Turn up the heat.

The angel is the snake is the sword. & with their help we move from unconsciousness into consciousness. From Darkness to Light with the use of Fire. In Zosimos' Vision we see

> The dragon or serpent represents the initial state of uncon-
> sciousness, for this animal loves, as the alchemists say, to dwell

"in caverns and dark places." Unconsciousness has to be sacrificed; only then can one find the entrance into the head and the way to conscious knowledge and understanding. Once again the universal struggle of the hero with the dragon is enacted, and each time at its victorious conclusion the sun rises; consciousness dawns, and it is perceived that the transformation process is taking place inside the temple, that is, in the head. It is in truth the inner man presented here as homunculus, who passes through the stages that transform the copper into silver and the silver into gold, and who thus undergoes a gradual enhancement of value.[14]

The Work is Ourselves.

The Hero kills the snakeheaded monster & becomes conscious but Medusa has wings now.

"Finally," from Burckhardt,

the snake/dragon alone can represent all phases of the work, depending on whether it is provided with feet, fins or wings, or is without limbs whatsoever. It can be considered as able to live either in water, air or on the earth, and, as salamander, even in fire. The alchemical symbol of the serpent thus closely resembles that of the Far-Eastern world-dragon, which first lives as a fish in water, and then, as a winged creature, soars into heaven. It also recalls the Aztec myth of Quetzalcoatl, the plumed serpent, which successively moves under the earth, on the earth, and in the heavens.[15]

The feathered serpent becomes the Morning Star. Opens its wings and soars up from the depths of Mexico. From Lawrence's *Plumed Serpent* came the solemn, impressive voice of Ramon:

I am the Son of the Morning Star, and child of the deeps.
No man knows my Father, and I know Him not.
My Father is deep within the deeps, whence He sent me forth.

He sends the eagle of silence down on wide wings
To lean over my head and my neck and my breast
And fill them strong with strength of wings.
He sends the serpent of power up my feet and my loins
So that strength wells up in me like water in hot springs.
But midmost shines as the Morning Star midmost shines
Between night and day, my Soul-star in one,
Which is my Father whom I know not.
I tell you, the day should not turn into glory,
And the night should not turn deep,
Save for the morning and evening stars, upon which they turn.
Night turns upon me, and Day, who am the star between.
Between your breast and belly is a star.
If it be not there
You are empty gourd-shells filled with dust and wind.
When you walk, the star walks with you, between your breast
and your belly.
When you sleep, it softly shines.
When you speak true and true, it is bright on your lips and
your teeth.
When you lift your hands in courage and bravery, its glow is
clear in your palms.
When you turn to your wives as brave men turn to their
women
The Morning Star and the Evening Star shine together.
For man is the Morning Star.
And Woman is the Star of Evening.
I tell you, you are not men alone.
The star of the beyond is within you.
But have you seen a dead man, how his star has gone out
of him?
So the star will go out of you, even as a woman will leave a man
if his warmth never warms her.
Should you say: "I have no star; I am no star,"
So it will leave you, and you will hang like a gourd on the vine
of life
With nothing but rind:

Waiting for the rats of the dark to come and gnaw your inside.
Do you hear the rats of the darkness gnawing at your inside?
Till you are as empty as rat-gnawed pomegranates hanging
hollow on the Tree of Life?
If the star shone, they dare not, they could not.
If you were men with the Morning Star.
If the star shone within you
No rat of the dark dared gnaw you.
But I am Quetzalcoatl, of the Morning Star.
I am the living Quetzalcoatl.
And you are men who should be men of the Morning Star.
See you be not rat-gnawed gourds.
I am Quetzalcoatl of the eagle and the snake.
The earth and air.
Of the Morning Star.
I am Lord of the Two Ways— [16]

This is the Serpentine Way of the Seraphim.

There are no biographies, no conclusions. Altho even as I finish Kris in all innocence brings me a lapis stone.

The Angels don't help us in the work, they are The Work.

It is up to us in our spiritual work to be watchful of the Angels, of The Work.

As The Dhammapada warns: "Watchfulness is the path of immortality; unwatchfulness is the path of death. Those who are watchful never die: Those who do not watch are already as dead."[17]

Sometimes it takes a fiery snake to sting us real good to make us watchful. Sometimes cooled by Angel Wings.

This is The Serpentine Way.

These are necessary Angels.

BACHELARD AND THE ANGELS

JOANNE STROUD

In the realm of the empyrean, Gaston Bachelard is a non–conformist. His angels bear no theological imprint. He has been called, perhaps not unfairly, a "pagan." As a twentieth–century devotee of the history of science, he was concerned primarily with images of elemental matter. When in mid–career his philosophical focus shifted away from the empirical, he began a search into the imagination and will, those two quintessential human faculties, which absorbed his latter career. His explorations convinced him that will and imagination, even when misguided in application, even when caught up in carnality, bear a quotidian relationship to the aspiring, higher side of human nature, that part which yearns for metaphysical meaning. This connection is a linkage, however tenuous, between the pragmatic Bachelard and the metaphysical fraternity of angels.

To Bachelard, the chief characteristic of imagination is mobility, and will, far from being a static "faculty," enters into and empowers any action. The definition of will as something akin to ego does not satisfy him. He insists that will includes an almost instinctual responsiveness to challenge and a characteristic surge of psychic energy. The loci of one's will and imagination provide fundamental insights into personal character and determine the teleological direction of one's life. This is a vitalist doctrine which he espouses, suggesting that life processes are determined by the dynamics of the interaction of will and imagination more than by purely mechanical means.

This coupling of foundational human characteristics to angelhood, in becoming more than a mere polemic outreach, is a concomitant of his basic philosophy.

Indeed, Bachelard sees angel images as pervasive in art, literature, philosophy, and theology, and therefore as integral to our cultural inheritance. He finds their appeal revealing. An angel's wing, like a bird's, symbolically exemplifies human desire for mobility, a transcendence of the earth–bound. Angels shuttle back and forth between the natural and the supernatural, ethereal messengers echoing the human yearning to bridge two realms. Their invisible presence is more powerful and numinous to the imagination than the visible. They are part of Bachelard's world of "the unreal" through which the real is delineated, the unconscious through which consciousness is grounded, the invisible through which the visible is defined. Even the vernacular of today—"winging it," "lightening up"—brings into metaphorical play what Bachelard describes as humanity's ever–present upward yearning. It is a yearning based on human need, the need to break Gulliver's threads, to soar free like angels.

Through imaginative borrowings from Swedenborg, Balzac, and Villiers de L'Isle–Adam, Bachelard builds his pastiche of literary images. A soaring wing opposes the downward drag of gravity. A luminous, astral light reflects transparency and inner insight. He exploits even the ubiquitous quality of the angel: it unites androgynously the best of the male and the female.

Always, images play upon the human will, galvanizing us into action beyond mere conscious acts of volition, forcing us into interaction with the world, driving us to be masters of it, ultimately to transcend it. Bachelard ascribes to the earth a will of its own, one in continuing contest with the human will. Similarly, the natural world is imbued with both soul, *anima mundi*, and spirit, *spiritus mundi*, which challenge the individual soul and spirit. This titanic competition whets humankind's thirst for improvement, moving always on an upward trajectory, always along the path of the angels.

In *The Right to Dream* Bachelard emphasizes that to become effectively spirit humankind must be "a will straining toward its destiny; it must be a will to youth, a will to regeneration."[1] It is straining toward a never-to-be reached goal which he calls "superhuman becoming." In psychology we relate this urge toward youth and regeneration to the *Puer* (or *Puella*) *Aeturnus* complex exemplified by Eros, who in the late Greek pantheon is a daimon with both dark and bright angelic qualities. Eros brings desire, or perceived need, into human lives, thereby fusing the longing urge. But the son of Aphrodite struggles with maturity and the need to accept responsibilities for his actions. He yearns to remain free, unshackled, able to fly home to the security of mother at the first sign of trouble from Psyche. The dynamic action epitomizes the awakening between love and the soul in search of liberation, probing new boundaries, and aspiring always to transcend them.

Bachelard implies that the pursuit of transcendence is a fundamental human urge that moves us *pari passu* with the angels. In doing so he differentiates between the will to verticality and the will to the horizontal, which shackles us to the purely practical. The urge to ascend or descend on an axis of verticality governs our moral judgments in the use of spatial metaphors to describe the reach upward to a higher nature or downward to a deepening of the dimensions of personality. In *Air and Dreams*, Bachelard explains the principle of ascensional imagination:

> Of all metaphors, metaphors of height, elevation, depth, sinking, and the fall are the axiomatic metaphors par excellence. . . . They govern the dialectic of enthusiasm and anguish. . . . It is impossible to express moral values without reference to the vertical axis. When we better understand the importance of a physics of poetry and a physics of ethics, then we will be closer to the conviction that every valorization is a verticalization.[2]

The ascensional imagination is always waiting to be activated. When we climb a mountain, upward desire, the will to ascension impels us: "the most physical kind of ascension is thus a preparation for the final assumption."[3] The thrill of attainment commingles with fear of the fall, or the fear of the abyss. Bachelard says: "We take part in imaginary ascension because of a vital need, a vital conquest as it were, of the void."[4]

Typically in a dream when we rise in imaginary flight, the abyss which before felt as if it were grabbing at our heels begins to lose its terror. Bachelard explains the dynamics:

> Let us for a moment experience dynamically this dominance over the chasm: we notice the abyss loses its distinctive features because we move away from it. One who ascends sees the obliteration of the abyss' characteristics. For him the abyss dissolves, becomes hazy, and grows more obscure.[5]

Bachelard contends that in our dreams we never imagine ourselves with angel–like wings until we have already mastered the art of flying: "Anyone who flies feels that he has wings when he need no longer make an effort to fly."[6] Slyly perverse, he suggests that wings on the heels are more effective than wings on the shoulders and that even the god Hermes has to use pediform attachments when off on an aerial jaunt. He observes that Michelangelo has only to lift the foot of one of his painted seraphs to suggest the ability to fly and that artists generally portray angels as if they were swimming in the firmament. Somewhat disdainfully, he notes that Leonardo da Vinci painted only mechanical, exterior wings, whereas Dante has no need for such props; his angels fly without the specific image of wings. He can render interior wings.[7]

It is in his preface to Honoré de Balzac's *Séraphîta* (1955) that Bachelard specifically discusses his approach to angelology. Here he underlines Balzac's direct and indirect borrowings from Emanuel Swedenborg, the eighteenth century Swedish philosopher who speaks to all those who respond to the angelic call. Commenting on *Séraphîta*, he says:

> A couple of pages may be enough to endorse the innate Swedenborgian enlightenment, to lend confidence to those direct, native impulses that launch human nature on an unwaveringly vertical course. Balzac had within him, as "engram" of all imaginary ascension, that Swedenborgian dynamism.[8]

It is the "unwaveringly vertical" urge that unites Balzac to Swedenborg, Bachelard to them both, and humanity with the angels.

Bachelard along with Balzac finds Swedenborg's angelic depictions fascinating. In an absorbing chapter of *Heaven and Hell*, Swedenborg asserts that "Each Angel Has a Perfect Human Form," eyes, ears, nose, etc. Each is a single person and a part of heaven: "Man, too, to the extent that he accepts heaven is also a recipient entity, a heaven and an angel."[9] Only blind ignorance sustains the belief that angels are incorporeal, airy creatures with intellects but without form. He finds intellectuals and the clergy particularly guilty of this skepticism; simple people cannot be so easily misled, since they could never comprehend anything that had no form: "That is why the angels carved or painted in churches are invariably represented as people."[10] To Bachelard, Swedenborg's vision "solidified the creatures of heaven"[11] by depicting the dynamics of vertical ascension, by sensitizing the reader "to approach each image in its quality as departure, as magnet for ascension, as standing invitation to an aerial future."[12]

Unlike Bachelard, Swedenborg claims through inner vision, through his spiritual eyes, actually to have seen angels. He writes:

> This is in the spiritual world, while everything physical is in the natural world. Like sees like because it is made of like material. Further, the body's organ of sight, the eye, is so crude that it cannot even see the smaller elements of nature except through a lens, as everyone knows. So it is still less able to see things above the realm of nature like the things in the spiritual world. However, these things are visible to man when he is withdrawn from physical sight and his spirit's sight is opened. . . . It is how I have seen angels.[13]

Swedenborg's angels are in a state of radical innocence: "What is true cannot be bonded to what is good, or vice versa, except by means of innocence."[14] Innocence is the acceptance that all knowledge is derivative and the willingness to be led like a child by the Lord. This finds an echoing, non–theological chord in Bachelard, who stresses opening our eyes to see the world with a child's awe and innocence, not with the naïvete of inexperience—as with Dostoevsky's Prince Myshkin, for example—but rather as a celebration of the earth's wonders. It is an innocence that is beyond ego, a post–heroic mode. There are no tasks, no goals, no work to accomplish, only the acceptance of the paradisiacal state of mind. It results from aspiring to the good, the true, the beautiful, and discovering it within oneself as well as externally in the world.

Bachelard finds the nearest approach to angelhood in human form in Balzac's novel, which he describes as "a poem of will, a dynamic poem"[15] and a "meditation upon the regeneration of human nature by the will."[16] Unlike Eastern meditation on being, it is the emphasis on "supernatural becoming," or "the human being's destiny of transcendence"[17] that is the central theme of *Séraphîta*. Notice the play on the name Séraphîtüs/Séraphîta as the androgynous near–angel protagonist. Séraphîta, the embodiment of the perfected creature, has no world–saving mission to accomplish. She has male and female qualities so complementary as to constitute near self–sufficiency—a divine amalgam of the sexes contoured in a human form. As a symbolic bridge between the sexes, she is viewed through different prisms—as a male by young Minna but as a female by the male characters. She is also a link between mortal and spiritual worlds, the synthesis in Bachelard's view "of earthly being and immortal being."[18] Thus she approaches the state of androgynous angelhood in mortal form. Bachelard's emphasis suggests by implication the ultimate possibility of attaining perfectibility in the human realm.

Bachelard invariably uses epigrams to emphasize his main points. In his preface to *Séraphîta* he augments his theme with an epigram from Villiers de L'Isle–Adam's *Axel*:

> Fulfill yourself in your astral light! Come forth!
> Reap! Arise! Become your own flower![19]

To fulfill one's being with astral light means fulfilling one's spiritual potential. "Superhuman becoming" is the soul's straining to become spirit. Success depends on the intensity of this urge toward the ascensional, toward angelhood. Bachelard extols the virtue of Dante as "the poet most attracted to verticality."[20] He likens this quality to the same force within Balzac and Swedenborg, "the profound traces of which Balzac urges the sympathetic reader to discover within himself."[21] Always we can resonate with the imagination of a poet. Thus it is through a new definition of, a redefining of participation mystique, through participation in the "psychic lyricism" of the poet, that we can join with imagination and will in the soaring significance of the angels.

ANGELS AND THE APOCALYPSE: H.D.'S TRIBUTE TO THE ANGELS

EILEEN GREGORY

As our gathering in celebration of angels draws to a close, it is fitting that we recall images of the last things, in which the angels' raucous music announces a moment of radical epiphany. Lest we sentimentalize these couriers, we need to remember their association with "the day of wrath," with strife, rage, blinding annihilation, with a terrifying spiritual economy.

> Grace be unto you . . . from the seven spirits which are before his throne. . . . [Revelation 1:4]

> And I turned to see the voice that spake with me. And being turned, I saw seven golden candlesticks. And in the midst of the seven candlesticks one like unto the Son of man, clothed with a garment down to the foot. . . . His head and his hairs were . . . white as snow. . . . And he had in his right hand seven stars. . . . [Revelation 1:12–16]

> And out of the throne proceeded lightnings and thunderings and voices: and there were seven lamps burning before the throne, which are the seven Spirits of God. [Revelation 4:5]

> And the seven angels which had the seven trumpets prepared themselves to sound. [Revelation 8:6]

> And I went unto the [seventh] angel [who held the open book in his hand], and said unto him, Give me the little book. And he

said unto me, Take it, and eat it up; and it shall make thy belly bitter, but it shall be in thy mouth sweet as honey. And I took the little book out of the angel's hand, and ate it up; and it was in my mouth sweet as honey; and as soon as I had eaten it, my belly was bitter. [Revelation 10:9–10]

We will return soon to these seven candle–lamp–angel–stars and to this bizarre scholar's fantasy of a square meal. But I'd like to contemplate with you today not the literal end of the world, the ultimate term, as faith might prescribe, but the nature of apocalypse itself and the angels ministering within it, as these arrive within the temporal frame of our own lives. There is never a dearth of those who tell us, echoing John, and calling to mind his phantasmagoria of cataclysms, that the end is at hand; apocalyptic fires may flare up intermittently in our imaginations, and not without reason, because something in us senses that it is possible, that seeds, hidden in time, may blossom in blood and fire—if we are at all awake to omens and portents. For as Tom Moore has said about annunciation, apocalypse too is an utterance, a script, or an open book to which one must carefully attend; it is a gift ministered by no mortal hands. I do not mean by apocalypse the destructive events themselves, but rather the moment of visionary revelation within destruction. Though this is an extraordinary moment, it may happen within ordinary life. Indeed it is a mistake to imagine apocalypse as a "far–off divine event." The world comes to an end more than once in the lives of most of us—bridges falling down, collapse and emptying, angry aftermath, shattering ruin—and within the ruin something waits to be seen and heard and read and recorded by newly–tempered senses.

Apocalypse is an uncovering or unveiling of a mystery which is hidden or obscured in time. If we take the account in the Bible as a paradigm of this moment, the angels (with brazen trumpets) instrument this revelation. Apocalypse comes to us, though not always and not necessarily, at moments of catastrophe or cataclysm, at times of shattering or breaking apart or ending or completion. And—distinct from the ample and benign tonality of the Annunciation—it comes from within the experience of great bitterness. It reveals to us, as John's vision does, the old and the new, the old which is being destroyed, the new coming into creation ("Behold, I make all things new [said he upon the throne]" 21:5). Yet in apocalyptic vision, such change from old to new is understood not in its gradual Sunday–morning form, but rather with its full dimension of shock and terror. Moreover, apocalypse is not merely a happening passively endured; it suggests an active, participatory, and critical engagement. Such a revelation of the hidden or concealed is made possible "by the expedient of obtaining a point of view from which it can be seen in its true significance (*apo*—removal from a place; *kalupto*—to envelop, to conceal, to darken)."[1] Apocalypse suggests a vantage point outside the temporal moment from which its signs can be interpreted. This momentary standing–outside does not come naturally; it appears to come as a gift, witnessing to a strength and amplitude seemingly beyond our powers.

In regard to this gifted moment of vision, help me for a moment to take up the little book held open in the hand of the seventh angel. What does this image suggest? Because somehow, especially to those like us to whom books are eminently edible, this image has a striking resonance. First of all, I am struck by the connection of apocalypse with the whole realm of the scriptable and the legible, suggested by the centrality of the Book in John's testimony, and by the various dictates to John at certain points: Come and read! he is told. See this and write in a book that others may read! Look at this but don't write it down! And once one takes this meditative path, don't we think of apocalyptic utterance in its essential form as the writing on the wall? (A moving hand writes on Belshazzar's palace wall—fairly unintelligible words—and Daniel interprets). "Blessed is he that readeth," John says. Writing and reading, like those images of script in the pictures of annunciation that Tom Moore spoke of, suggest apocalypse as another moment of germinal communication, somehow outside the ephemeral flow of attention. More simply, in apocalypse all things seem cryptic, as though part of a hidden language; things present themselves in the guise of legible signs which, though obscure, are so forceful as to demand their transcription and transmission.

It is, I believe, this compulsion upon the reader to *process* apocalyptic signs that is suggested by John's metaphor of eating. "I have eaten at the hand of angels," they say, but *books* as angelic food? In regard to the human gestation of divine language, apocalypse is distinct from annunciation: in annunciation the golden words enter the ear of Mary and then her womb; in apocalypse, they enter the guts and bring a bellyache. The image of eating the book comes from Ezekiel, though in that source Ezekiel's book is sweet only, not bitter. The book John accepts is "In the mouth sweet as honey, but in the belly bitter"—easy to take in, murder to digest. In fact, these angelic papyri make of the belly something like an alchemical alembic: a cauldron of bitter salts and syllables.

I am led to these meditations through the work of H.D. (Hilda Doolittle), a twentieth–century American poet. H.D. lived most of her life in London, and like so many writers of her generation she experienced the two devastating world wars firsthand. She was in London during the bombardment in World War II, and out of her suffering of these events came a remarkable series of three long poems—*The Walls Do Not Fall*, *Tribute to the Angels*, and *The Flowering of the Rod*. These comprise one work finally published as *Trilogy*.[2]

I'd like to muse with you a moment about these poems, spiritual meditations on the shattering nature of war, as a way of understanding the manifestation of apocalypse in our lives and the angels that minister to it. (It is interesting to me that *Wings of Desire*, the contemporary re–imagination of the presence of angels, is set in Berlin, within the weary memory of terrible war and destruction). War is one of many forms of the breaking of the vessels, to use a metaphor from Kabbalistic spirituality. In the Jewish Kabbalah the fractured nature of human existence came about as the result of the overflowing of divine light into vessels too rigid to contain it: as H.D. speaks of it, the "invasion of the over–soul into a cup / too brittle, a jar too circumscribed" (WDNF 31). According to tradition, those insufficient vessels shattered into shards' and fragments, and their integrity must be restored by arduous spiritual exercise.[3] So too there is an element in human cataclysm, such as war, which represents not wholly the descent of darkness, but, paradoxically, a spilling of light—or perhaps, from the human perspective, an inextricable confluence of light and dark. In other words, catastrophe is itself the evidence of divine Presence, with all its ambivalent power.

H.D. powerfully gives this sense of the devastation of war as a divine event, and following her meditation we may grasp something of the character of apocalypse. The conflagrations in sky and earth, the brilliant terror of the exploding bombs, shatter the brittle case, the husk of self. The divine character of the cataclysm does not in her vision represent divine retribution (still the commonest, most pervasive understanding of human catastrophe), but more specifically it signals an "uncovering," bringing with it a mysterious sense of revelations, of grace moving within the rubble of lives, of presences within the rubble of buildings. Yes, angels within the devastation. H.D. knew the angels well (Gustav Davidson acknowledges H.D.'s help in his compilation of *A Dictionary of Angels*). H.D.'s poems represent a subtle and original exploration of the angels within apocalypse. In exploring this territory H.D. is, like Daniel, a reader of the writing on the wall and, like John, an eater of bittersweet books. But in some crucial ways H.D. reads and writes with a consistent resistance to the tradition, modifying the images that comprise our experience of the angelic dimension—persistently calling into question the sufficiency of some of those very images that we have explored during this conference.

The first book of the *Trilogy*, *The Walls Do Not Fall*, opens with the startling image of a mythical apocalypse—"over us, Apocryphal fire"—but with the image of literal apocalypse or uncovering as well: sealed rooms broken and sliced open to unveil and expose the poor, arcane, though sacred world within. H.D. was in Egypt in 1923 when the inner chamber of King Tutankhamen's tomb was unsealed, in London in 1940 through 1944 when its buildings were suddenly shattered in the many waves of German bombardment. The poem begins with superimposed images from Egypt and London. Only fragments of wall remain, ruins; there are no doors: and one finds something uncanny, H.D. suggests, in

this exposure of interiors, and in one's ability, like ghosts, to walk
through walls.

An incident here and there,
and rails gone (for guns)
from your (and my) old town square:

mist and mist–grey, no colour,
still the Luxor bee, chick and hare
pursue unalterable purpose

in green, rose–red, lapis;
they continue to prophesy
from the stone papyrus:

there, as here, ruin opens
the tomb, the temple; enter,
there as here, there are no doors:
the shrine lies open to the sky,
the rain falls, here, there
sand drifts; eternity endures:

ruin everywhere, yet as the fallen roof
leaves the sealed room
open to the air,

so, through our desolation,
thoughts stir, inspiration stalks us
through gloom:

unaware, Spirit announces the Presence;
shivering overtakes us,
as of old, Samuel:

trembling at a known street–corner,
we know not nor are known;
the Pythian pronounces—we pass on

to another cellar, to another sliced wall
where poor utensils show
like rare objects in a museum;

Pompeii has nothing to teach us,
we know crack of volcanic fissure,
slow flow of terrible lava,

pressure on heart, lungs, the brain
about to burst its brittle case
(what the skull can endure!) (WDNF 1)

Within this superimposition of images of opening and uncovering, the poet points to important spiritual and psychic aspects of apocalypse. One notes, first of all, the communal, rather than the private or esoteric, nature of this revelation: it belongs to "us" as a common knowledge: "we passed the flame: we wonder / what saved us? what for?" The cataclysm makes evident the inclusiveness of human fragility. Moreover, one also becomes aware of the presence of time in a fresh way, one's place within the long human recording. Apocalypse makes evident the "writing on the wall" like the hieroglyphics within the exposed Luxor temple. That writing, strangely, does not signify doom and destruction. On the contrary, the signs, now seen as within a sacred space, declare what endures eternally within devastation. The "Luxor bee, chick and hare / pursue unalterable purpose," hieroglyphs suggesting fertility, regeneration, the action of rising.[4] Signs, the ordinary signs of the human world which now seem uncanny, "continue to prophesy"; and in this shattered yet strangely sacred world, without roofs, doors, or walls, the ordinary barriers and thresholds between inner and outer, the "Presence" announces itself. Like Samuel or the Delphic Pythian, one is captured by sacred utterance. The image of the unsealed inner chamber, at once holy and mundane, wherein the intimate arcana of daily life is exposed in a slice of time, is of course a metaphor for the shattering of the self, for the unveiling of the soul before its necessity. Apocalypse brings the knowledge of

"Pompeii": awareness of hidden fury and bitterness ("slow flow of terrible lava"), awareness of the old petrified life frozen in stone.

Throughout *The Walls Do Not Fall*, in the midst of cataclysm, are these moments of uncanny Presence bringing awareness of the old desiccated life and the necessity for transformation: "The Presence was spectrum–blue, / ultimate blue ray, / / rare as radium, as healing; / my old self, wrapped round me, / / was shroud" (WDNF 13). And in the midst of the devastation, one senses the presence of wings:

> but when the shingles hissed
>
> in the rain of incendiary,
> other values were revealed to us,
>
> other standards hallowed us;
> strange texture, a wing covered us,
>
> and though there was whirr and roar in the high air,
> there was a Voice louder,
>
> though its speech was lower
> than a whisper. (WDNF 12)

John says that he "turned to see the voice that spake with me" (1:12)—for in the economy of apocalypse one can see voices and hear visions—and so too does H.D. turn to see this intimate voice speaking within the hiss of incendiary. In the second of the long poems of *Trilogy*, *Tribute to the Angels*, H.D. fully acknowledges the angelic presences within cataclysm and fully assumes the analogy of war with the apocalypse—the destruction of the old, the epiphany of the new. This poem is the poet's gift or tribute specifically to the seven spirits/candles/lamps/ stars before the throne of God, the seven angels of the Presence who instrument the Apocalypse. (H.D. calls these seven spirits, variously named within tradition, Azrael, Gabriel, Raphael, Uriel, Annael, Michael, and Zadkiel.)

Throughout this poem H.D. recalls the Apocalypse of John because, within this shattered world, she has visions, through the modest annunciations of dreams and daily occurrences, of "a new heaven and a new earth." H.D. insists upon this vision at the heart of apocalypse, which, in her poem as in John's, is a vision mediated by angels. To understand the emphasis which H.D. gives, we might recall what John says about this "new heaven and the new earth," the "new creation," the "new Jerusalem," the "Bride of the Lamb" (21:1–23). In John's Apocalypse the vision refers, implicitly, to the city at the end of time, marking the close of human history, a place where no pain and no evil dwell, the exclusive city of those whose names are written in the Book of Life. John witnesses that the city is foursquare, that its walls are of jasper, that the city itself is of gold, "like unto clear glass," that the twelve foundations of the walls are of precious jewels (sapphire, emerald, beryl, topaz, amethyst . . .), and that "the city had no need of the sun, neither of the moon, to shine in it: for the glory of God did lighten it, and the Lamb is the light thereof" (21:23).

John's hyperbolic visions are so strenuously elaborated within Christian iconography that they seem almost literal in their constraint upon imagination. At the same time they are strangely provoking. So forceful are John's images that almost any vision of the "last things" is a re–vision, despite John's admonition against free–play of interpretation ("If any man shall add unto these things, God shall add unto him the plagues" [22:18]). Harold Bloom comments, in regard to John's Apocalypse, that when one declares a work closed, "Of its lateness, you have made an earliness," necessitating a lineage of revisionism.[5] The same is true of the angels: the Church acknowledges the names of only three angels, while within tradition the names of the angels are legion. In this regard I'd like to make clear an issue which we have not directly confronted in this conference: to speak of one's own apocalypse or revelation is to dwell on the boundary of heresy, at that place where what is known and prescribed buckles, wavers, and dissolves in entering the territory of the unknown; it is to dwell, in Don Cowan's phrase, "at the Veil."

Individual apocalypse stands at this heretical edge, and H.D. goes out of her way to emphasize that edge, affirming the authority of John's Christ, who says "Behold I make all things new," while ironically puzzling over John's claim that his is the only legitimate record of revelations. Throughout Tribute to the Angels H.D. reveals a steady resistance to John's insistences. As mystics have always asserted, her visions are simple and new; they are like but unlike any described in any tradition; they are discrete, belonging distinctly to this soul, and only this distinctiveness constitutes their truth, though, paradoxically, they belong to all. In one of the first sections of *Tribute to the Angels* the poet echoes the last section of *The Walls Do Not Fall* to evoke the image of the "new creation" while quizzing and qualifying the given Biblical images:

> Your walls do not fall, he said,
> because your walls are made of jasper;
>
> but not four–square, I thought,
> another shape (octahedron?)
>
> slipped into the place
> reserved by rule and rite
>
> for the twelve foundations,
> for the transparent glass,
>
> for no need of the sun
> nor moon to shine;
>
> for the vision as we see
> or have seen or imagined it
>
> or in the past invoked
> or conjured up or had conjured
>
> by another, was usurped. . . . (TA 2)

H.D.'s *Tribute to the Angels* looks first to the miracle that the "walls do not fall"—not literally the walls of bombarded London, but the walls of the inner chambers, revealed within destruction as eternal. Her guide (Hermes) tells her: "Your walls do not fall, he said, / because your walls"—like those of the New Jerusalem—"are made of jasper." H.D., then, in revising John, will witness that the city of her apocalypse is the soul itself, revealed within time, within the transmutations of the ordinary, within dream and waking dream. In her witness the visions of John (and other visions of the Old and New Testaments) must be claimed by new lights, in new contexts, within a via negativa of traditional iconography.

Tribute to the Angels begins with the summoning of Hermes, the patron of alchemists (and of "orators, thieves and poets"), partly because H.D. here submits iconographical language itself to a hermetic process of occult transmutation. The poet seeks to renew the religious traditions which have become petrified and fragmented, especially in time of war. She prays to Hermes: "collect the fragments of the splintered glass // and of your fire and breath, / melt down and integrate, // re-invoke, re–create / .opal, onyx, obsidian . . . " (TA 1). But the transmutation of language suggests at the same time the transmutation of soul. The patron of alchemists is needed because in this poem the experience of apocalypse takes place within an alchemy of war, whose primary materials are bitter salts. He who "makes all things new" is also the governor of strife and violent process:

> but I *make all things new,*
> said He of the seven stars,
>
> he of the seventy–times–seven
> passionate, bitter wrongs,
>
> He of the seventy–times seven
> bitter, unending wars. (TA 3)

The alchemical process, intricate and ambiguous, is variously discriminated within hermetic tradition; indeed, one of the fascinations of alchemical science is the instability of attempts to systemize that process, since alchemical speech is essentially poetic in its obliquity, its slippages, evocations, superimpositions, and associations. In this sense Hermes is indeed the patron of *Tribute to the Angels,* for the linguistic mode of the poem is alchemical in this way; and, subservient as they are to the immediacy of vision, the alchemical images in the poem are themselves obscure, unsystematic, self–concealing, one means among many of approaching expression of the inexpressible.

Essentially, the alchemical process, according to tradition, consists in the breaking down or the "blackening" (*nigredo*) of the *prima materia* in order to distill and crystallize rarer substances and finally to crystallize the "jewel" or the "living stone," an image of spiritual and psychic integrity. The whole of *Tribute to the Angels* meditates upon the mysterious jewel coming into being. Out of the mortifying alchemy of war what is crystallized is not the first white or innocence, the first virginity of Mary at the Annunciation, but what the alchemists called the "second whiteness" or "white earth" of the albedo, the virginity and innocence to which one arrives after the process of mortification.[6] After that "whitening" comes a final mysterious moment (glimpsed at the end of *Tribute to the Angels*), the "reddening" (*rubedo*), representing the process of embodying spirit within body and desire. The alchemy of language and of war is also in H.D.'s poem the alchemy of angels: they are primary guardians of the mysterious changes wrought in imagination, in body, heart, and mind. The transmutation of the jewel, the chief sign for the alchemical process throughout *Tribute to the Angels,* is instrumented by or is coincident with the epiphanies of angels in the poem, each of whom bring discrimination to the process of purgation and temperance.

The opening of *Tribute to the Angels* is dominated by bitterness and despair: "Not in our time, O Lord, / the plowshare for the sword . . . not in our time, O King, // the voice to quell the re–gathering, / thundering storm" (TA 4). But within the cacophony and emptiness of "unending war" arises a voice recalling the presence of the angels. Of the seven angels only two gain prominence in the poem—Uriel and Annael—

---

becoming the central powers within the soul's arduous death and renewal. The first is Uriel, "the fire of God," the angel who, the book of Enoch tells us, "watches over thunder and terror."[7] In a sense he is the instrument of the brilliant destructive confla–gration, but the instrument too of the brilliance manifest within. Never before, the poet says, in Rome or Jerusalem or Thebes (the great doomed cities) have so many witnessed the collapse of the world, as

> the lightning shattered earth
> and splintered sky, nor fled
>
> to hide in caves,
> but with unbroken will,
>
> with unbowed head, watched
> and though unaware, worshipped
>
> and knew not that they worshipped
> and that they were
>
> that which they worshipped,
> had they known the fire
>
> of strength, endurance, anger
> in their hearts,
>
> was part of that same fire
> that in a candle on a candle–stick
>
> or in a star,
> is known as one of seven. . . . (TA 6)

These witnesses of and martyrs to the conflagration do not, like the damned souls in John's Apocalypse (6:15), hide in caves from the "day of wrath." They do not assume themselves to be victims of divine retribution. Rather, that divine fire in the heavens is their fire and wrath: their anger and willful endurance draws its strength from the very angel of the cataclysm. The bitterness and fury of the apocalyptic conflagration is a spilling of divine light: in the sky, in the soul, it is a generator, a grounding of the alchemical process.

Indeed, *Tribute to the Angels* is from first to last a meditation upon the necessity of anger, the urgency of the soul's affirmation of its own distinct bondage in bitterness. The transformation of the jewel, signaled by the epiphany of Uriel, begins with the distillation of bitterness, in the recognition that bitter salt (blood, sweat, tears) is at the heart of life and transformation.[8]

> Now polish the crucible
> and in the bowl distill
>
> a word most bitter, *marah*,
> a word bitterer still, *mar*,
>
> sea, brine, breaker, seducer,
> giver of life, giver of tears;
>
> now polish the crucible
> and set the jet of flame
>
> under, till *marah–mar*
> are melted, fuse and join
>
> and change and alter,
> mer, mere, mère, mater, Maia, Mary,
>
> Star of the Sea,
> Mother. (TA 8)

In this alchemy of soul, at the same time an alchemy of language, one's single salt is fused with the greater—mere common salt is "fused and joined" with mer and mère, the salty first ground of feeling and desire. This distillation of salt creates the first moment of the jewel, the "Bitter,

bitter jewel / in the heart of the bowl." This is a crystallization of the distinct pain of the soul given at birth and always carried, "this mother–father / to tear at our entrails" (TA 9).

But the recognition of bondage implicit in the "bitter jewel" arouses rather than satisfies longing. Another angel is needed as the necessary companion and counterpart to the bitter fury of Uriel—Annael (Haniel), the peace of God, identified with Venus.[9] Her quiet presence is first recognized in the poem through a glimpse of the luminous light of Hesperus (Venus) in the standing water of a furrow. The poet then recognizes the necessity of a further alchemical work moved by another form of divine fire: "Swiftly re–light the flame, / Aphrodite, holy name . . . return, O holiest one, / Venus whose name is kin // to venerate, / venerator" (TA 12). The erotic presence of Annael/Venus signals a change in the jewel: it now "lives . . . breathes"; it is richly animated, a mysterious and complex manifestation. The transmutation of the jewel here, as in the alchemical opus, is signaled especially by changes in color, which are now inexpressibly subtle: "green–white, opalescent, // with under–layer of changing blue, / with rose–vein" (TA 13). These colors echo the "green, rose–red, lapis" of the opened Luxor temple. They hint at a mysterious richness of experience, while the specific shades of green and blue suggest the movement from *nigredo* to *albedo*.[10]

The epiphany of Annael occurs through the simplest and quietest of images—vivid in its beauty precisely because it accompanies the violence of Uriel—the image of "a half–burnt out apple–tree / blossoming":

> we asked for no sign
> but she gave a sign unto us;
>
> sealed with the seal of death,
> we thought not to entreat her
> but prepared us for burial;
> then she set a charred tree before us,
>
> burnt and stricken to the heart;
> was it may–tree or apple? (TA 19)

This may–tree or apple tree flowering in the heart of death and decay is "delicate, green–white, opalescent / like our jewel in the crucible" (TA 17), and like that image of the jewel, this moment of presence is inexpressible—though, paradoxically, not because it is arcane and exclusive, but because it is common:

> This is no rune nor riddle.
> it is happening everywhere;
>
> what I mean is—it is so simple
> yet no trick of the pen or brush
>
> could capture that impression;
> music could do nothing with it,
> nothing whatever; what I mean is—
> but you have seen for yourself
>
> that burnt–out wood crumbling . . .
> you have seen for yourself. (TA 21)

This moment of apocalypse belongs to all, the poet insists, a sign of the moment of fresh life emerging from fiery and complete death, which each knows in a distinct way. It is also, clearly, the sign of an angel—"it was *the Angel which redeemed me*," the poet says, echoing Abraham at the moment of his death (Genesis 48:16). But this angel does not appear with brilliance and with glittering wings—but with modest luminosity and ordinary grace.

As one manifestation of the "Star of the Sea" and as the phosphorescent light of Venus, modulating the jewel toward mysterious color, Annael ushers in the central vision of the poem: the experience of "a new heaven and a new earth" manifest in the epiphany of a Lady. Just as the poet engages in the ritual of paying tribute to the angels, one by one "in the sequence of the candle and fire // and the law of the seven," as she has just summoned Gabriel of the moon cycle, a dream interrupts the procession: a group of friends are gathered,

---

EILEEN GREGORY

159

> when we saw the outer hall
> grow lighter—then we saw where the door was,
>
> there was no door
> (this was a dream, of course),
>
> and she was standing there,
> actually, at the turn of the stair. (TA 25)

How odd, someone says, "she is actually standing there, // I wonder what brought her?" (TA 26) Then the poet realizes she has been dreaming, that the luminous light of the Lady in the dream is actually the phosphorescent face of a ticking clock. But when she awakes, the Lady is still present, even more than before.

Who is this Lady? Here, as elsewhere, the poet must attempt to move awkwardly beyond known language and images to express the simple enigma of this familiar figure. She does this by entering into a dialogue of sorts with the sophisticated reader who knows religious iconography and hastens to homogenize any fresh religious image with yet another layer of traditional interpretation. Just as H.D. does with Biblical precedents, so with these obscuring traditional overlays, she accepts while at the same time qualifies the given images, firmly correcting the glib response. "We have seen her / the world over," the poet says, "Our Lady of the Goldfinch, / Our Lady of the Candelabra, // Our Lady of the Pomegranate, / Our Lady of the Chair" (TA 29)—all those Our Ladies in "every imaginable" posture, with infinitely various props and accompaniment. "But none of these, none of these / suggest her as I saw her" (TA 31), the poet says. For "she bore // none of her usual attributes; / the Child was not with her" (TA 32). The poet tries to approximate the impression of the Lady by appropriating Biblical images of brilliance; in a deliberate, revisionary gesture the woman's vesture is compared to the whiteness of Christ's robe at the Transfiguration (Mark 9:3)—"her veils were *white as snow,* // *so as no fuller on earth / can white them*"—and to the whiteness of the Son of man (He of the

seven stars) in Revelation (1:13)—"*she was clothed with a garment //
down to the foot*" (TA 32).

This figure of brilliant whiteness comes as the supreme vision
within the summoning of the angels. She is and is not herself an angel,
because the poet says she is "nearer than Guardian Angel / or good Dae-
mon" (TA 39). She is a presence, an actual one, but indefinable in any cat-
egories of experience—not Santa Sophia, or the Holy Ghost ("the SS of
Sanctus Spiritus"), or the New Eve, or "a symbol of Beauty . . . Our Lady
universally," or she of "the seven delights . . . and of the seven spear
points" (TA 36–37). In resisting the pat formulae which somehow miss
the particular mystery of the Lady, the poet suggests her significance. She
prefaces her meditation on the Lady by alluding again to the New
Jerusalem of Revelation, "there was // *no need of the moon to shine . . .*"
(TA 41). The further, deliberate comparison of the Lady with the transfig-
ured Christ and with the Son of man suggests that she carries in herself
these revealed images of redeemed presence:

> I grant you her face was innocent
>
> and immaculate and her veils
> like the Lamb's Bride,
>
> but the Lamb was not with her,
> either as Bridegroom or Child;
>
> her attention is undivided,
> we are her bridegroom and lamb (TA 39)

The Lady's love exists within no complex triangulation with Son and
Father; "her attention is undivided." Within the poem the Lady is the
vision of the redeemed soul, the New Jerusalem of the Apocalypse, "Psyche, the butterfly, / out of the cocoon" (TA 38). She is the epiphany of the
alchemical Bride or the second whiteness, the soul transformed through
destruction and suffering.

In H.D.'s revelation the Lady too, like the seventh angel of the apocalypse, is carrying a book. Why a book? the poet asks. Perhaps because "she is one of us, with us," or perhaps because she gives tribute to those of the book, the word and image, those of the brush and quill, to that timeless communication of the word. Even here in this latter day vision, apocalypse is connected with the legible and scriptable. But the Lady's book does not describe the tangent of past error leading to calamity ("You have been measured and found wanting," as Daniel interprets the writing hand on the palace wall). It is not the final, exclusive Book of Life:

> she carries a book but it is not
> the tome of the ancient wisdom,
>
> the pages, I imagine, are the blank pages
> of the unwritten volume of the new. . . . (TA 38)

This book is neither bitter nor sweet: it is not to be eaten, not to be read and interpreted, but to be inscribed within new gestures of the soul.

The vision of the Lady brought about through the guidance of the angels, especially through Uriel and Annael, issues in the final transmutation of the jewel, a mysterious glimpse beyond attained whiteness to the point "where the flames mingle // and the wings meet," to the moment of a fullness of color, like that manifold jewel of a city in John's vision:

> I John saw. I testify
> to rainbow feathers, to the span of heaven
>
> and walls of colour,
> the colonnades of jasper;
>
> but when the jewel
> melts in the crucible,
>
> we find not ashes, not ash–of–rose,

> not a tall vase and a staff of lilies,
>
> not *vas spirituale,*
> not *rosa mystica* even,
>
> but a cluster of garden–pinks
> or a face like a Christmas–rose. (TA 43)

The final moment of this apocalypse, and this testimony of an apocalypse, is once again a differentiation, separating the new images from those others given in tradition. John's grand vision of ultimate change and of infinite and eternal containers—the "span of heaven" and the heavenly city—is contrasted with the gradual and arduous change of the jewel in the fiery crucible. In this context, the refined and sophisticated images of virginal purity (*vas spirituale, rosa mystica*) are not at home, but rather the homely epiphany signaled in ordinary flowers, with the suggestion, in the "face like a Christmas–rose," of the nativity, the delicate new child coming at the end of the process of rebirth. Moreover, the poet suggests the final moment of alchemical change—beyond the white of ash and lilies, the faint and delicate beginning of the reddening in pink and rose.

Apocalypse brings fiery change, *"lightning in a not–known, / / unregistered dimension,"* opening one to the uncanny inner world where there are no witnesses, no records, no maps, *"no rule of procedure."* Within this space the angels minister: *"for even the air / / is independable, / thick where it should be fine / / and tenuous / where wings separate and open"* (WDNF 43). The angels, H.D. suggests, navigating one within the very marred and violated landscape of destruction, confirm the necessity of marring bitterness as well as of mysterious patience. They do not counsel escape from the tortured mind and body into another purer and more ethereal world, because "from the visible / there is no escape; / / there is no escape from the spear / that pierces the heart" (TA 22). Psyche resides in this wound, in the fiery crucible, in the "flowering of the burnt–out wood." And in a briefly attained moment of peace and pleasure, she reflects our gaze with "a face like a Christmas–rose."

ANGELS AND ART

ANGELS COME IN THE SPACE BETWEEN

LYLE NOVINSKI

In this reflection on angels I want to offer three considerations. The first is from my teaching at the University of Dallas, the second is a parable drawn from my life, and the third is a presentation of the angel in my work at St. Rita's Church in Dallas.

This first reflection comes from my teaching, wherein each year for many years I have worked with the images of the length of the history of art, bringing before me in a continual stream the images of man's making, and thus the reflection of the thought of those times. The character of our presentation of what we call sacred has had a long fascination for me—so that as I work through the long thread of time each season, certain things leap out at me, call attention to themselves by their presence, or by their change. Angels are just such a subject. One cannot help but see them change, alter, reflect the character of our sacred presentations, as the time thread moves past.

All things float in Byzan-tium's golden domes (Fig. 1). Within a gold–lined space feet turn down, giving us a *vertical* view of the foot's instep usually understood as a *horizontal* form. Weightless figures, human in our dimension, overlap feet in ways not hostile, but, at best, uncomfortably

Figure 1

close to poorly mannered. Unaccustomed we are to such a manner, and even remembering the power of Byzantine Hierarchy, do anyway ponder this denial of firm footing. Taken as a whole though, we do understand that such a device serves to inform all viewers that boundaries of time and space have been crossed and human weighted measure does not apply.

Art lives in the reflection of another world, one in which our measure is denied by forms that float. Bounded by this sense of being other, all things portrayed are not of our senses, not measured by touch, sight, or space. This formal world cannot be confused with our own, and its acceptance makes a clear separation between what is there and what is here. If it is in art, fresco, mosaic, or metal enameled book cover, it is not of our place. There is power in all of this and freedom as well—the power given to things unseen, and the freedom to see the unseen as real, a reality that does not require the proof of touch. Freed from measure's constraint the hand rejoices and makes for our other–knowing splendid things. The divided and subdivided image of the angel is part of that freedom, and part at once of showing the splendor of things that are not seen. Memory itself taken from the arcaded frontal of a sarcophagus, where stories are

Figure 2

told of the plan of salvation, becomes embroidered, en-larged, enriched, until on the frontal of San Marco, the *Pala D'Oro* (Fig. 2) contains an imaged essay in gold, arched and enameled, encompassing all within itself. Here an object becomes a catalogue, miniaturizing and collecting in its enfolding recesses the symbolic gathering of all memory into one object. Assent is required for this, belief in ways in which large stories can be compressed into gathered symbols, and the enjoyment back on the senses of the splendor of these symbols taken together. The senses are within and without at once. Things made manifest beyond sense measure, and the senses delighted in the presence within our world of images of such complexity.

In Byzantine art, the senses rejected and the senses embraced are placed in a tension that has no distance between. The same object announces both concepts and holds them fast within itself. Drawn and repelled in our being, we are held fast, attracted and rejected; we find our stasis. And so do the angels.

Within this stasis there can be no change, no movement, and space has no value for things are coexistential.

The icons of the world pay tribute to this understanding, being of two worlds at once. Centuries of little change in the images of the divine attest to this simultaneity, the coexistential of the perception of two natures.

Somewhere in childhood memory an elder said, "Fools rush in, where Angels fear to tread" and we all knew what that meant. I think now, that one could also say, "When Angels tread, only a fool would not fear." For Angels will tread, we shall see, and when they do so at our bidding, something will be lost.

They stand on clouds eventually (Fig. 3), but that was not required at first. Giotto required at first that their robes fit over their wings, and having once

Figure 3

Figure 4

admitted himself to the game of charging numbers to a pinhead's space, moved us a little away from the Angels as a portion of the price for seeing the divine more clearly. We ought to be pained by the spilling of blood the fresco says, as pained as were the angels on Calvary's darkening afternoon, wherein they fly about, rending their garments (Fig. 4), and borrowing our human anguish for our own example. Angels measured are angels supposed I fear, and supposed angels must stand somewhere and clouds are as good a

Figure 5

place as any. The world moves toward measure in a rush, arming angels, armoring them and placing them on cloud stasis, making them quite like us in many ways, the mystery to more clearly see.

Like we might be, jewel covered and laden, about God's bidding in jewelled certainty they come. Like Van Eyck's jewelled annunciation, we are announced and made present in this moment of incarnation (Fig. 5). We and our measure, our eye and our weight, are brought to be, remembering on the zodiac of the floor the season's mystery at the same time. The symbol enters the world, and in its entrance disappears within.

I do not think it goes away, or dies; it is placed within for our finding.

Gruenewald (Fig. 6) re-speaks what Giotto said in an earlier century, speaking of the pain, though there is no room for the angels to announce our pain in concert. His vivid crucifixion is without space in its black sky, but fully engages our sense measure in cataloguing the possibilities for pain. For a world that has asked for the measure of God's knowing of human pain, and which has asked to see the divine proven more

Figure 6

clearly, Gruenewald has given us a powerful image. When we open the wings to another panel, he reminds us as well of what that visibility has cost us. Here are the angelic beings catalogued for us, the kinds of Angels which we cannot see, reflecting in their splendor and surprise for us, the opposing possibilities of the pictured demons and the truly fallen.

Italy's deep–spaced and measured knowing cannot supply such diversity, but charges us to see angels more like ourselves (Fig. 7), and being like ourselves, to place their feet on firm footing, casting shadows from the new subjectivity, as a shifted universe of sun–centered knowing.

Figure 7

The symbols warp, the halos narrow, and the Angels tell us of the distance the space between has become. There are reasons for the thinness of angels in a Byzantine world—the distance between the felt and the known was very thin. God's insulation from us, the angelic layer, was too thin for angels to turn in without folding like creased paper.

Should I think, within my world, where the angels might be, I would look for the space between things, looking at a world where is and ought are different; I would look for the space, and see who is there. If there is a here and a there, if there is a we and a they, who is between? What do those between say? Do those between bear the misshaping measure of the distance between as we have made the images of angels bear? When I see a warped halo painted, or a wing sleeve sewn in for an Angel's undressing ease, I know there is room for angel work, for these creatures are well–between, and bear the unshaping forced by the sundering of a coexistential world.

A language of location has grown up to describe this sunder as a normal geometric location (Fig. 8). On a diagonal away from our frontal view is the other, the layer of spirit we say, —It is over there, you just have to connect the point here with the one over there, behind, just a little to

Figure 8

the right, or a little to the left, it would seem. Should we connect all the points, those in front of us and those we know in differing locations behind, we will have all things tethered, connected, and in place once more. Such forms, restitched together of sundered portions, recall the face of a Frankenstein, a stitched image of sundered parts, given life in the connecting.

If we see little difference, assume that the face of one is over the face of the other, we may see angels, thin, transparent, reveling in jewelled brilliance, celebrating the stasis of a known correspondence.

THE SECOND REFLECTION is from my life. It is titled "Parable."

"My grandfather came from the Ukraine, Russia I think," he said, in response to my question of the origin of his name. It sounds Polish, like mine, though it depends on where the border was, when. My great grandfather's funeral card lists him as having been born in what they called the Polish province of Germany.

The lad, sandal footed, wearing warm weather white, and fresh from the shower, was seated on a bench to my right, on a rise above the chapel, and had surprised me a minute or so before with his greeting, "This is a good place, you know."

I stopped in my walk and recognized him as one of the students who had walked through the city with me the day before, as I toured a bus load of high school students about our city streets, part of a program of recruiting and orientation to college.

It was a bright morning, just about noon; I had come from Mass that morning and was crossing the campus on an errand, walking up the short walk from the Chapel to the Mall when his voice had stopped me. It had been a thoughtful Mass; about the congregation were faces I recognized from the Saturday walk, and I had wondered if I would see Michael at Mass that morning. Michael, the athletic Ukrainian, had worked to the head of the line as we crossed and recrossed streets and had easily talked with me as we moved along. There were comparisons with Cleveland, his home, and Dallas. There was surprise at the newness of everything here, and at the absence of trash, and of people on a Saturday afternoon. We were touring an empty city, speaking of its life which was unseen, for all the workers were not here at their work, though their tables were set on the sidewalks for lunches and parking lots prepared with landscaping for their cars on another day. Around a particularly appointed tower with bronze statuary, pools of water, and blooming flowers in low bowls he responded: "I know what this is, it is an executive Disney-land." "Yes, I suppose it is," I said.

Of the sixty or so students, you wonder how many will return for the fall session, and enter the university, join your life in learning and work. I wondered at Mass about Michael, would he be here today, and would he be here next year. It was a passing thought, for my thoughts were really on my work and learning for the next year, and the years after. There were lumpy things in my present, dissatisfactions with work, and the pattern, structure of faculty and administrative life here on campus. I was asking the right questions of myself, in the right place for me. In this chapel I had made many things, influenced its spaces, and read well its symbolic life, containing my own in its framework. I was surrounded by my family and students in a place I had helped form, pushing back thoughts of change and reordering, some dark and vengeful before my own white altar. In prayer the decision came to stay, to live with the good, and to work around the bad, reset the pathway, reorder the pavers, and goodness in feeling followed.

I left the chapel, left my family for another car, for my errand of some kind. Pondering my decision to continue I took a single route up the hill toward the Mall when I heard the voice on my right.

"This is a good place you know."

THE THIRD REFLECTION comes back from my work as an artist. In this case the work is executed in stained glass; it is the Angel of Paradise, seen here in this watercolor cartoon made in preparation for the windows of St. Rita's Catholic Church in Dallas.

The Angel here is the last figure in a cycle that begins with Paradise, and with Adam and Eve in the garden. The cycle is a cycle of time, salvation history above our heads, following a typical program which starts with Genesis and moves through subjects of windows drawn from Exodus, Prophets, Incarnation, Public Life, Resurrection, Pentecost, and finally Paradise, where the human figure is returned to Paradise by this guiding angel with great brilliant wings.

In this space we inhabit one zone and these stories another. The only contact between the space of the floor and the space of the windows is found in the Genesis window, where the gaze of the Adam and Eve pair is downward, to us in our terrestrial zone. This is proper for a Genesis that is written as a story of the fall, making of this image the first of a series that exists in time, as we do, and placing the paradigmatic stories parallel with our journey below. This journey ends in death, and is then joined with the image of paradise overhead. The stories, in their placement, are oriented to the cosmic forms, conforming in their placement to the movements of the heavenly bodies. Easter is most brilliant at the spring equinox, Incarnation and Pentecost respond by moving from light to dark, being darkest at Incarnation, and moving to full light at the summer solstice, Pentecost.

The windows are a cycle above us, recording the character of the cycle of life and its overlay with the plan of salvation. It is stated in time from the beginning, and closes with our consciousness in death, where the angel figure bears us away.

Unlike the spatially definite iconographies of our post–renaissance past, these images place man in time rather than in place. Our participation is on the floor of the church, where our place is fluid and temporal. The paradigm of that temporal life is the continuous passage overhead, which is united in form and light with the cosmos for our direction.

ARTISTS' ANGELS

MARY VERNON

I have felt the uncomfortable honor of having been depicted as an angel (by my friend Carole Scholder). I know the compliment is mixed, in some way, for a mortal. Might it be that Carole intends to remind me how far I am from the angels?

Fra Angelico, aptly named, painted angels with confidence, and painted them in the conventional form, as ethereally beautiful young male teens, perfect women/men in luxurious robes, with wings of jewels and fire. They move gracefully, with never a flawed silhouette. From the *Linen Guild Tabernacle* of 1433 to *The Annunciation* at San Marco in the late 1430's, Fra Angelico's angels are the convention I measure the rest against and often find the rest wanting.

The convention within which Fra Angelico worked is said to have arisen among Jews, before the time of Christ, from Assyrian images of winged gods and spirits. We can see the Assyrian image in the British Museum in alabaster reliefs from Nimrud (Khalku) of *Ashurnnashipal II Worshipping the Sacred Tree* (c. 883–860 B.C.). These handsome, winged things are bearded like men and coiffed and combed like kings. Or it may have been that the old Shemitic religion, whose spirits dwelt in fields, stones, fountains, trees—in natural phenomena—gave them to a single God who ruled all.[1]

Finding the source of the convention seems not to be enough. It leaves out the thing I think closest to revealing an angel's being and real work—the ancient Egyptian image of the Ba, a part of the soul. In tomb papyri such as the New Kingdom *Scroll of Ani*, the Ba hovers over the mummy on its funerary bed. The Ba has a blue hawk's body, a short, black tail, and a human head, goateed and short–haired. In his little, yellow claws the Ba carries the ring of eternity. While I do not pretend to understand the many constituents of the soul known to the Egyptians, I see what they mean about the Ba as opposed to the Ka, the life–support–bound soul segment. A Ka in a person, or in a god–king, or in a universe–sized god requires nutrition. It can't hold where the body fails. A Ba, not particularly attached to physical nutrition, flies in close range, hears and wants, pushes and tells. Maybe it is a "will." But I cannot help thinking of it in terms we use more commonly as "gumption." Perhaps psychic gumption. Among the Egyptians, whole creations are often said to have souls. If the universe has a soul, its Ba, its psychic gumption is angels. That seems the universal way to think of them.

In Giotto's frescos at Assisi, when God grants the stigmata to St. Francis, God appears to Francis very much in the device of a Ba. God hovers with a Christ–like head, outspread arms, human hands and feet, and a body wrapped in the wings of Thrones (six rose wings, two up, two out, flying, and two down, covering His legs). I do not suggest that the Christian God and Bas or angels are the same things, but rather that the Christian God, and His angels as well, wear the wings of the Ba in a pose of divine intent, as if the drive and will of God to get things done could be shown in the winged thing.

This cosmic gumption, or will, or universal intent, or moving inspiration, appears in the work of modern artists all the time. The fact that the image is no longer the conventional winged boy of religious pageants makes no difference. What truth could our eyes find in the conventions we have discredited? Cosmic gumption stalks around powerfully in such things as Umberto Boccioni's *Unique Forms of Continuity in Space* of 1913. The inevitable forces Boccioni saw in modernity are very like angels. If we want them to fly rather than stride, we can find in Jean Arp's string reliefs of the late 1920's silhouettes—wing–armed, casual, floppy, superbly "cool" amoebae—floating by. In a Jackson Pollock pastel, ink, and gouache of 1945, the scratchy strength of making a psyche visible looks like an angel to me. We have not stopped sculpting and painting them; in general we have just stopped knowing them.

I confess, I love the old convention too. On Ghiberti's *Gates of Paradise* at the Florence Baptistry, three gowned, winged men speak to Abraham. They act in the old tradition (derived from Byzantium) that the Trinity manifested itself in this way. The three creatures of heaven who speak to Abraham signify the three aspects of God. It is a way to see the Trinity without forcing the Trinity into physical bodies. The convention employed by Ghiberti has rules, rather unstable rules. Angels have human heads and bodies (which may not need feet), and wings. They act. To Abraham the angels are ambassadors in a symbolic number. To St. Hilary (at St. Hilaire, Poitiers, ca. 1130 A.D.), two angels are the hands of eternity reaching into the death chamber, carrying off the naked soul to heaven. One school of thought (especially strong in nineteenth–century academic training) insists that a splendid angel must be a good, big one with wings powerful enough to carry him in flight. Lord Leighton painted this angel species, as in *Elijah in the Wilderness*, where the angel looms over the handsomely muscled prophet and sports a wing span capable of flying in a Jeep, should Elijah need it.

I have always preferred the opposing school of thought within the Western convention—the one that sees angels as a species only slightly related to man, the angel species being beautiful, small, uniform, innocent. This puts the burden of performance and the need for nobility on the race of human beings, where it belongs. I think we are more crude and much more promising, at our best. You see this vision of the angel at its grandest in Hugo Van der Goes's *Portinari Altarpiece*. All the angels are the same pallid genius, very small, looking like Woody Allen with long hair. They differ in vestments, perhaps by duty. They are far too pure to take on (or to need) the heroic task of stumbling toward a union with God, the task of the lowest men in the altarpiece. Another Northern European painter of the Renaissance, Matthias Grünewald, shows the angel at its greatest variety (within the European convention). In his *Isenheim Altarpiece*, angels serenade the Virgin and Child in the central panel. Under a gazebo of fantasy, the singers, iridescent, with human–like, bird–like, and animal–like faces, play all the instruments of the day. Some are the size of hummingbirds. Some are the size of teenagers. Some are lit from within. In contrast to Grünewald's attainments, easy conventions such as Bouguereau's nineteenth–century angels simply bore everybody.

I must mention that Europe produced a convention of wingless angels too. One sees them in the sculpture of Flaxman (as in *St. Michael and Satan*, 1822, in the Victoria and Albert Museum); they look confusingly like Herculeses and Perseuses. This well–intentioned idea stems from the convictions of Michelangelo, who thought wings a travesty on a beautiful body. Whether he was correct in thinking we could see angels outside conventions remains a subject for interesting discussions.

When I have drawn angels in my own work, the wings of flight and fast movement have always been there. Boccioni's are not the wings of birds, nor are Arp's. Pollock needed no bodies, halos, or gowns. But I have been intrigued by the convention. And so, for this conversation, I have decided to reverse it for you.

Perhaps only to humanity can an angel be a man with bird–like wings. This is said by human beings to combine the ultimate natural intelligence (ours) with the ultimate natural swiftness (flight). What if the angel were a bird with our arms?

PRACTICAL WORK WITH THE ANGELS

GROWING WINGS

GAIL THOMAS

What does it mean to "grow our wings?" I want to suggest that we all have wings, waiting to sprout. We are wanting to grow our wings. We begin to feel the stirrings, the roots spreading out, creating a tension within us.

We know, of course, that to grow wings is to be carried by spirit, to be moved by joy. Angels *are* joy! Angels move *through* joy, the joy of creation, of drawing the essence of the being they are working with into its most brilliant potential! Angels are transformers—mediating the vital essence of each one of us into forms that best express our unique being. And not only for us, but angels do their work on everything that takes form—each plant, blade of grass, flower, shrub, tree, as well as crafted things—a building, and yes, an institute, and yes indeed, a city.

It is the essence of angelic beings to bring the vibrations of physical life into form. Angelic life is in open atonement with divine essence and patterning. When we say, "It is God's will," we are implying a pattern of divine consciousness over all things. It is the angelic beings who bring this patterning into place.

In these times of enormous change, here at the end of the 20th century and the beginning of the 21st, the spiritual realms are opening to us. We seem to be recognizing the profound transformations taking place in each one of us, in our work, in our institutions, and in our awareness of planetary citizenship. And, while so much of the institutional life we have known is breaking down, most of us sense that we are being guided, that there is an ultimate form in chaos. All creation stories say: "In the beginning there was chaos!" We begin to see the imprint of the divine attempting to be born anew. Given the continued speeding up of the changes taking place, it is no wonder that there is such an explosion of interest in the phenomena of angels.

Dorothy Maclean was one of the founders of Findhorn Gardens. She learned to hear the voices of the angelic realms and wrote down what they said to her. She calls this her "God Voice." McLean wrote the words she received from the deva of a certain shrub in Findhorn Gardens. "Deva" is a Sanskrit word meaning "the shining one," or "being of luminous light." In angelology, the word deva is used for beings who oversee the plant and mineral world, and "angel" is used for the human realm. Hear the shrub deva's words:

> "We fly on the wings of joy, for we could not manipulate forces if we were weighted down like humans. We start plants off by whirling forces into activity, and the joy in us has a constant movement which we pass on in our work. What fun it is to hold each little atom in its pattern!"

Let us imagine what is going on here. We are seeing two distinct worlds within every given thing that has form. William Bloom identifies these two worlds in his *Devas, Fairies and Angels*. One world is of matter which, we know from our physics, vibrates within its living sphere of atoms. The other world is the angelic one, which, as carrier of the divine consciousness, forms an envelope of sorts over and around the vibrating atoms, wrapping and drawing them, magnetically, into the shape which they desire to be. This "desire" is the key; it is an inner imprint. The tulip knows it is to be a tulip and not a rose. The vibrating desire to be a tulip is there within the bulb. It is the work of the angelic being to "hold each little atom in its pattern" and this envelopment, this holding, begins to form the tulip's shape. As the tulip yields to the guidance of its angel guardian, it begins to grow its wings, the petals form on the stem. The petals are its wings! And after the wings are formed, the color comes. What a mystery this moment is—the gathering of color into the blossom! The color celebrates the vital life essence of the tulip. It announces the miracle of co-creation.

Angelic consciousness is at all times connected with cosmic awareness. It cannot be otherwise. We might imagine it as a direct stream of light emanating from the fullness of Divine Consciousness. It knows instinctively cosmic proportion and patterning, not from a superimposed, prescribed blueprint, but from a matrix of possibilities within a given archetypal field. We can sense within the depths of our being that our angels know what we want to be.

Most of the angel material agrees that angels grow in consciousness from association with us. The devic world, also expands in consciousness in association with the mineral and plant worlds. So, we are growing in awareness together. This expansion is a part of the action of growing wings. As the angelic consciousness expands in relationship with us, we begin to feel the "stump of the wing swell" as Plato puts it. Plato says it is the soul within the human that grows the wings. He puts it this way in *Phaedrus*:

> The natural property of a wing is to raise that which is heavy
> and carry it aloft to the region where the gods dwell. . . .

And Plato describes the actual moment of growing the wings, saying the soul responds to the experience of joy:

> . . . by reason of the stream of beauty entering in through his
> eyes there comes a warmth, whereby his soul's plumage is fos-
> tered, and with that warmth the roots of the wings are melted,
> which for long had been so hardened and closed up that noth-
> ing could grow; then as the nourishment is poured in, the
> stump of the wing swells and hastens to grow from the root
> over the whole substance of the soul, [until] the whole soul was
> furnished with wings. Meanwhile she throbs with ferment in
> every part, and even as a teething child feels an aching and
> pain in its gums when a tooth has just come through, so does
> the soul of him who is beginning to grow his wings feel a fer-
> ment and a painful irritation.

What is intriguing about Plato's image is the notion that the wings are always there, they always have been. "With that warmth, the roots of the wings are melted, which for long had been so hardened and closed up that nothing could grow." It is the warmth that melts the roots of the wings. My sense is that it is the warmth flowing from the intention of our hearts that melts our wings. When we "in-tend" we stretch toward something. We experience desire, and if it is desire aimed toward the beautiful which always manifests from the divine, it warms us.

I want to say a few things about desire. My sense is that *desire* is *always* protected by angelic presence. The desire within each of us is our intention, our inner longing to grow our wings. Now, do not confuse desire with lust, with envy, greed or covetousness. Desire springs from our inner imprint, from our soul-self that knows who we can be. Desire draws our colors to us. So we must examine closely our desire. We have been taught to be ashamed of our desire. People say to us, "Just who do you think you are?" Well, who is it that you think you are? Who do we want to be? This question is our life-work. It deserves the full service of our lives.

When we grow our wings, wings seem to grow everywhere! Robert Bly says in his book, *Iron John*: "If a human being takes action, the soul takes action. . . . The soul itself does nothing if you do nothing, but if you light a fire, [the soul] chops wood; if you make a boat, [the soul] becomes the ocean." The two streams of being—the physical and the angelic—weave together a gossamer wing. Once we see from our winged perspective, everything else seems to have elevated with us. We say "Imagination soars, it takes flight!" And God gives this promise: "I shall give my angels charge over thee. To keep thee in all thy ways." ("All thy ways. . ." This includes what we *desire* to be!) "And they shall bear thee up, lest thou dash thy foot against the stone." (We are promised protection for what we desire to be!) But we must cooperate. We must do our part. My sense is that our cooperation is in our recognition of the angels, that they are, indeed, all around us. It is in our in-tention, that is, in our stretching out, in our allowing what we desire to *warm* our hearts that the root buds of our wings begin to melt.

THE MATERIAL HALF OF THE ANGEL:
SILENCE NARRATIVES IN THE MYSTICAL
EXPERIENCE OF THE LOSS OF FREEDOM

THERESE SCHROEDER-SHEKER

At first this presentation[1] may seem to be composed of disparate members. It has something to do with fire and something to do with light, something to do with Guardian Angels and something to do with the Seraphim. It has something to do with the wilderness of chaos, something to do with contraction and expansion, and most of all, something to do with silence.

Part of the birth or remembering of my higher self began to take place as a rhythmic and disciplined activity in the act of singing. Because I have been trained as a harpist, it never occurred to me until quite late that I could or should sing (in concert) and suddenly a whole world was opened up. Previously I had loved and learned and embraced instrumental repertoire in a very, very deep way, but I did not sing in concert, only in prayer. The challenge was to bring the quality of prayer into that professional life, make the interior exterior, and transform it in multiple ways.

While still in a very formative stage, my teachers told me that there is so much great music that we should never perform and never record music unless we *love* it. *Burning love* was the criteria. One teacher in particular taught about Madame Wanda Landowska's[2] belief, that we should never ever perform literature that had not already been "ours" for seven years. She suggested that the integrity of a great artist demanded that the music we were playing was no longer "out there," on the outside. We are to live in the experience of the music, till it becomes part of us, body and soul, skin and bones, living-streaming, before walking on stage. Somehow, this is not always possible in a modern context, but when I began to *sing* this literature I realized that when you sing, you step into someone else's shoes. You are singing someone else's story, and for a few moments or an hour, or for the period of time that you are singing, you carry their heartache or you wear their wings. Through singing people's stories I realized that you wear each other's vestments. You take in and on their soul experiences. You honor them. You recognize them. You pay attention to their story by caring enough about it to sing it back into existence. These accumulated stories are ways we can create bridges between one another and form relationships of love and compassion. Sometimes we can even rectify a moment, or an hour, or a period of injustice by singing about something that needs to be brought into balance. This is not to say that the pure instrumental experience is pale; it is simply different. Singing is a different physical, bodily, internal activity than playing an instrument with strings, keys, reeds, etc.

The greatest singing takes place when we observe periods of silence. You cannot talk or sing all the time and still expect to have something meaningful to give away. This observation of silence is crucial in identifying the split between concert artist and concert audience. A fragmentation exists; the two are asking to be one, but this is difficult to achieve. Silence is the key; our own inner silence must be allowed to be heard by the audience. We heal that split by transforming stage into altar and by an exteriorized performance into a vital, streaming inner-life that is made available, audible, to others.

Let us consider this discipline I am calling "preparatory silence" which I consider to be both purifying and strengthening. I have found several examples of extraordinary silence narratives. They have to do with mystical ascent, although they do not avoid the descent. These narratives are essentially maps of the mystical life. They are about personal burning and they are about voluntary silence. I am thinking in particular of both ancient stories and very modern stories. I begin with the Budaliget story[3] because it is the one I have taken into the entire fabric of my life as a rubric of *voluntary silence*. I take the stories from the book *Talking with Angels: Budaliget 1943* by Gitta Mallasz.

The Budaliget story is a startling 20th-century documentation of involuntary silence and the transformation that takes place through sacrifice. This story involves four young Hungarians (three Jews and one Christian), caught in the cross-fire of the Nazi occupation while living in the village of Budaliget. Three of the four eventually die martyrs' deaths in 1944 in the concentration camp at Ravensbruck after having saved the lives of some fifty-nine Jewish women and children. They were not political activists. They were individuals struggling with spirituality in a very dark time. They had seventeen relentless months of *spiritual resistance work* culminate in complete loss of physical freedom, a central collision with brutality, starvation, betrayal, chaos, cold, and deception. But somehow, despite their deaths—willingly accepted, their memoirs were preserved. What is essential here is that the memoirs remained hidden for thirty-three years, at which point the survivor and scribe, Gitta Mallasz, was interviewed on a French radio program. It took an additional seven years, adding to a total of forty, for the narratives to be published.

From the very heart of struggle and sacrifice, these four young people speak about being sustained in a series of dialogues with angels. The angels speak to them in a mystical chorus. They speak every Friday afternoon at three o'clock and continue in this way for the following seventeen months. Some of the most urgent angelic protocols follow:

> . . . The angel burns and says, *"In haste, you approach death from the fore. In lingering, you approach death from the rear. In acting at the right instance you know no death. Every true act springs from Love. The act at the right time is an act outside of time. Listen carefully! . . . Sound is Love! Turn your heads towards the never-before-*

*heard! The new voice is: Silence! There is a wonderful mirror in you
and it reflects the divine, but only in silence. If the mirror is not
clear, you cannot create. [In this silence] a new ringing will come,
and you are the bells. The silence I taught you is the sum of all the
mysteries. We teach you to sing. . . . Sing always! The angel lives,
acting through song. [This] silence is the house of the shining Word
in which Love burns. . . ."*

These three Hungarian prisoners of state suffer completely only to emerge from the literal flames with a genre of voice that governments cannot contain. The poet William Butler Yeats[4] describes that kind of voice as "the mystical fruit of the alchemical rose which transmutes the weary heart into the weariless spirit." At one point, before their capture and death, the angelic visitors described the purpose of their teaching: *to make us capable of enduring ever-more intense light.*

The key given to us by the angels is strong and clear. Light alone just disperses; it can blind us with its brilliance, but is fraught with illusion. In order to maintain equilibrium, we, in human form, need what is both luminous and proportionate. This guideline, *luminous and proportionate,*[5] was a standard used by Hugh of St. Victor, Thomas Aquinas, Bernard of Clairvaux, and others, in order to discern if an initiative was truly spiritual.

Let us continue with the Budaliget narrative. One of the three young people asks an angel, "What must I do to become one who forms this new integrity of body, soul, and spirit?" The angel responds,

"Burn . . . Burn, and heaven will be in you."

I would describe heavenly light as voluntary burning, voluntary sacrifice. Learning is a form of burning too, and wherever fire burns, true and false will be separated from one another. Later, an angel points to the area of our eyes saying,

*". . . Matter and spirit meet here, ignite, and radiate through the eyes.
From the throat to the eyes, matter becomes ever more subtle, but it is
still matter. Keep the way pure!"*

Even while practicing silence, we have the opportunity to find each other anew, through the eyes. For the mystics, hearing is receiving, drinking in streaming sources. Likewise, seeing is receiving, can become beholding—a conscious encounter where the physical sense of touch is transformed into the Grail sense of cherishing.

The one woman who survived to tell this story, Gitta Mallasz,[6] considered herself only a scribe and kept silent for thirty-three years. She gave it time. At one point, an angel told Gitta:

". . . Lips gone silent are not yet Silence. Be new vessels! Be Golden Chalices!"

Part of the miracle of this narrative is that four young people willingly gathered together to do something creative, luminous, and proportionate. They were willing to burn, spiritually; they did so as exemplars for the whole community. I see that the way they worked with angels is directly involved with incarnating spirit into matter. Listen:

*". . . Sound became body and was born. The body is Love which has
become matter . . . ."*

You cannot hear these stories and walk away without this part of the message. Their entire manner of burning was interior. First comes melting, then, what is unnecessary falls away, and form changes. All this, so that we may practice inner-emptiness (*kenosis*) and welcome and receive—welcome and receive spirit into matter. I see this as an incarnational spirituality that goes beyond our named institutional religious identities. It seems imperative for the twenty-first century. In these ways—refining, burning, reforming ourselves—we can all stand together.

Hold these images and realities close to your heart, while we move on to another chapter, this one a much less known narrative of silence and involuntary contraction. It is Ukrainian, and relates to a great natural law, as does Budaliget. This law applies to science, math, biological life, and the hermetic inner life. We know that biological growth alternates between rhythms of contraction and expansion, but so do many other kinds of growth (for example, musical life). We nurture our seeds in the dark, in the protective dark, in contraction. Then, with the right amount of time, in the silence, in the waiting, in the womb, in the nurturing darkness, seeds expand into the light. A musician also expands and plays in such a way that the receivers are quietly transformed; following the music, there is a necessary silence. We even take the music into our sleep.

Here is the secret: prolonged contraction necessarily results in elevation and expansion on the next level. It can do nothing else. Go to Woolworth's. Buy a ten-cent balloon. Inflate it fully. Hold it in your hands the way mischievous children do, smashing the bottom. The air that was caught in the bottom pushes itself up. It expands and elevates and this is also true of the human soul. In the case of Budaliget, the young people contracted—gave away—every part of their physical freedom, their voices, their bodies, and in the end, emerged as an integrated voice (a spirit ensouled) that bombs cannot destroy.

This story, placed in the Ukraine, concerns involuntary suffering, but it does eventually become conscious and voluntary. The incarcerated prisoners witness elements of their own resurrection bodies. They witness elements of a streaming incarnation of spirit into the matter of their own bodies because they volunteer to understand suffering in a new way. These compiled prison stories redefine the loss of freedom as *particularly concentrated and intensified living*. Writers, historians, poets, and scientists are often condemned to years of enforced silence in work camps, often for their unpublished thoughts. Prisoners of war begin to hear and respond to an inner voice that even affects the visible material world. The Ukrainian prisoner Phanine reports that if you concentrate on saving your soul, only then do you save your body, as a side benefit. Solzhenitsyn, too, says that only the spirit can save the body, and the loss of spiritual concentration (*burning silence*) leads to physical disintegration. In exploring the Soviet prison documents, the diaries of a Russian dissident named Andrei Sinyavski appear to be as complex and as vital as anything in the history of mysticism, and certainly equal to the angel messages of 1943 in Budaliget.

Sinyavski succeeded in smuggling his diaries out of the camp at Dubrovlag and published records of his "political silence" diaries under the pseudonym Abram Tertz.[7] He began incarceration as a self-described atheist and emerged as a mystic. His book relates to a particular kind of sacred song, *visionlieder*. Of course, the idea of the chorus is Greek and tragic, an exteriorized conscience. In Sinyavski's diaries, essentially letters to his wife Maria, the "chorus" originally reflects the endless conversations from the crowded barracks that penetrate his soul. As his transformation occurs, the chorus can be reconsidered as the collective voice of the ministering angels.

His book addresses the terrible underpinning of cold and loneliness, complete loss of freedom, isolation, and then the unexpected peace when one is utterly emptied. His freedom is born of obedience to his inner voice, the ensouled spirit, which cannot be taken away by an outside force. One loses this ensouled spirit, he says, *only by a personal act of betrayal*. He begins to write seriously about art and describes his art as his spirituality and says it comes out of silence. First, he works *through* the senses:

> . . . Art is not the representation, but the transfiguration of life. Table or forest is not an image. *Golden table* is. It is just like a tree growing and bearing fruit in the form of eyes. Art consists in the opening of the eyes . . . thereby endowing it with vision . . . a true image is akin to Transfiguration. . . .

His first steps deeply involve his own physical senses; he is an embodied, incarnational man. He then slowly begins to transform his senses. He receives the unbearable physical cold and he transforms it into warmth and light because of the power of his own soul. Other quotes from his diary:

> ... When the rain pours down endlessly, you can begin to feel quite cozy ... actually getting frozen and wet through, experiencing a lost sensation, enlivened only by tenderness. ... Let it rain. ... The snow falls day and night ... it falls quite soundlessly—like light. ... I find I can stand the bitter cold. ... When I was free I used to suffer a lot from the cold in the early evening ... when there is a feeling of death in the heart. ... Here it is not so ....

For him, sight, touch, and hearing are all inter-related and become organs of multiplicity. Over the seven years, the boundaries of his own physical body and his-body-to-other-bodies changes. His personal space is the universe, and he makes no mention of prison bars. Another quote:

> ... I have only one relative: God. ... Let everyone pass beyond the bounds of his life story! ... There must be plenty of room within us ... and our soul must be so spacious that we can wander through it and go down a staircase to the sea, and sit down on the shore and look ....

Seven years of enforced silence transform his previously materialist-realist world view as he enters into alignment with the initial hermetic tenet from the ancient Egyptian Emerald Tablet: "As above, so below." An incarnational spirituality embraces matter and spirit simultaneously and reinforms the way in which he communicates with words. His diaries take us to the threshold or perhaps the crossroads where both worlds intersect:

> ... Art is a meeting place ... of spirit and matter ... it converts matter into spirit and vice versa. ... I often sit down to write a

letter to you . . . just to touch a piece of paper you will be holding in your hand. . . . Art is created in order to overcome death,
but in a state of intense expectation of it, in the lingering
moments of farewell. . . . Art is always more or less an
impromptu act of prayer. . . . Because of the Spirit we are sensitive to the influence of all kinds of ideas—so much so that at
certain moments we lose our own language. . . . The Word for
us is such a substantial entity (spiritually) that it comes to
resemble a physical force. . . .

"'The Word' comes to resemble a physical force." This, to me,
becomes increasingly remarkable. In silence, Word becomes potentized, raised to the next level, as Logos. As constructions of time and
space fracture for the silenced political prisoner, his relationship to
body-within-time changes. He comments how little the men age despite
the extreme physical hardship and lack of nutrition. Previous values
fall away, and the notion of time is replaced with the experience of
eternity. Even though they are all emaciated and have shaved heads,
their faces reveal distinctively shining individualities. With their eyes,
they gleam silently into one another.

> . . . Time has stopped and we are flying inside a missile or an
> arc. . . . Space no longer exists here and since time is restricted
> . . . ephemeral earthly events are placed in perspective . . . the
> past was aware that beyond time there was eternity and they
> knew how to reveal its presence in every fleeting moment.
> How diminished people seem, once they are freed. . . . In the
> labor camps, people are literally preserved. Having come here
> as a boy, you can live to be an old man, yet still remain some-
> thing of an adolescent in your physical appearance. . . . Earth's
> time no more applies here than it does on Mars. . . . We don't
> grow old. When life is bleak and empty and clothes are drab,
> the human face requires the right to greater expressiveness . . .
> its allotted role is to make up for all that is missing . . . our faces
> enable us to lean out, as it were, from within . . . the face vio-
> lates the law of nature; every man is like a palace of crystal . . .

allowing light to pass both ways, back and forth, between spirit and matter. . . .

Such an extraordinary document! I must say, Sinyavski is rare. Today, he is a free man.

Consider the practical ways in which these silences, contractions, and stillnesses are carved out, wrung out of originally involuntary situations, and yet, they created new voices. Silence is not a vacuum; in making room for another presence, it can potentize sound, raise it to the next highest level in its transformation process. In the 20th century camps (work camps, concentration camps), the angels commanded the silenced to sing.

We also have these wonderful stories of the brave women in South Africa, the women of Capetown[8] and Pretoria. They do not want to be separated from their men—their sons, husbands, lovers, and fathers. Standing with their babies at their breasts before large armies of armed soldiers, they sing their freedom songs—defiant hymns in Zulu, Xhosa, and Sotho—the anti-apartheid songs. In doing so, they spiritually disarm the soldiers:

> . . . *Siyahamb' ekukhanyen' kwenkhos,*
> *siyahamb' ekukhanyen' kwenkhos.* . . .

> We are marching in the Light of God;
> we are marching in the Light of God. . . .

They stood in the hot blazing sun, covered their children's heads and looked right into the guns, singing:

> . . . *Siph' amandla Nkosi*
> *Wokungesabi*
> *Siph' amandla Nkosi*
> *Siyawadinga.* . . .

O God give us power
To rip down prisons
O God give us power
To lift the people. . . .

O God give us power
And make us fearless
O God give us power
Because we need it. . . .

They sang in antiphonal choirs until finally the soldiers put down their guns.

We have similar stories from World War II and the Warsaw ghetto. At one point, an entire group of Hasidic Rabbis is about to be shot. They are standing near a wall, aware that they are about to be executed. In pure response to the moment and attention to the spirit, they spontaneously begin to sing their prayers,[9] the Hebrew cantillations. The sung prayer, the last act of a lifetime, is so authentic and potentized that the Nazi soldiers are arrested at the soul level, put down their guns, and walk away.

Sometimes there is a Guardian Angel in the voice of the singer despite the lack of perfection. There is a very important quote from the 13th century *Zohar*[10] that we need to remember, concerning the fact that angels respond to human song:

> . . . It is also known and believed that those angels who sing by night are the leaders of all other singers; and when on earth we living terrestrial creatures raise up our hearts in song then those supernal beings gain accession of knowledge, wisdom and understanding, so that they are able to perceive matters which even they had never before comprehended. . . .

The angels can know us more intimately and love us when we sing, and they are not asking that we sound like the Philharmonic. They ask us simply to sing because we are harmonic. We are symphonic and in these ways we can connect with the angelic world. Clearly singing (and certainly singing of any sacred repertoire) changes everyone involved, the doers and the receivers. Song is the realm where matter and spirit marry. It is the realm of earthly and heavenly union where angels and humans work together. Joscelyn Godwin, commenting on Pseudo-Dionysius, also reminds us that the knowledge of the Seraphim cannot even be spoken; it can only be sung. It is the Seraphim who burn incessantly and their role is to sing praise, with ardor and rapt attention for all of eternity.

So the *Zohar* brings this mystical teaching full circle explaining that there is in fact angelic response to human song. They love to hear us sing. Our earth-bound souls must rise in heart-felt song whether in freedom and celebration or to transform a terrible moment of injustice in order to bridge heaven and earth. Angels and humans travel on ephemeral highways of light. These are the woven songlines of sacrifice and celebration. When we pay attention to these songlines we create a new nervous system, a metabolic nervous system for the earth within communities and beyond communities.

Gitta Mallasz says: "The angel lives, acting through song." I am certain this is true. The diaries of the poets and mystics and seekers of every time period show that humans have hungered for the companionship and the presence of angels from the beginning, and I suggest that there are reminders in popular music, despite the commercialism. I am remembering Aretha Franklin, and her hunger for the perfect companionship:

> . . . Gotta find me an angel . . . to fly away with me. . . .
> Gotta find me an angel, who would set me free. . . .
> A heart without a home. . . . I don't want to be alone!
> Gotta find me an angel: in my life. . . . [11]

And what about our modern day minstrel John Gorka? Of course, he's romantic. For him, the angel imagery and image of woman collapse into the same horizon. Longing for the place of our heavenly origin and longing for the lover become the same plea. He sings it from his heart:

> . . . I saw a stranger with your hair. . . .
> I saw another with your eyes. . . .
> I heard an angel with your voice.
> By the way, how is my heart?
> By the way, how is my heart? . . . [12]

He describes how this angel *flashes* before his eyes, *moves* through the crowds, feet never touching the ground, taking him *by surprise.* Just an angel in disguise, just in for a visit. One can easily doubt it, but as Christian Morgenstern says in a poem, I think we hurt the angels if we don't acknowledge their presence.

Remember the Four Tops? Listen carefully; see if you don't think an angel influenced this message:

> . . . Now if you feel that you can't go on,
> because all of your hope is gone,
> and your life is filled with much confusion,
> and happiness is just an illusion,
> and the world is crumbling down:
>
> Reach out! Reach out!
> I'll be there,
> with a love that will shelter you.
> I'll be there,
> to cherish and comfort you.

I think and feel that the angels wait for us at every given moment. I also believe whole-heartedly that we do not need to recreate a Budaliget or a Warsaw Ghetto or another Capetown in order to sing with fire, in order to potentize song, raise the voice and change what is chaotic into what is luminous and proportionate. If we alternate song and silence, consciously, with burning attention, every little chance we give them, every little wedge, every little moment, every corner of inner-emptiness and every rounded tone carves out the possibility to ring with them, to live with them, to bridge heaven and earth, to live in the material half of the angel.

A few more of the angelic protocols from Budaliget. They help us see what will come. They say:

> . . . *You will be tilled by endless searching.*
> *You are never alone. . . .*

Again, the angel says:

> . . . *It is your task to approach me.*
> *Raise your heart.*
> *What needs to be done has voice and you have ears to hear.*
> *Listen carefully! This ringing of bells is preparation.*
> *A new Ringing will come, and you are the bells.*
>
> *If you have faith, your burden wanes with the diminishing power of the moon. And your strength swells with the increasing force of the moon.*
> *Work with it; every force is an enemy if you do not love it. . . .* [13]

The ringing voice has a kind of body, weaves a kind of spiritual force, and it is ours with which to work. In singing, we ask for the incarnation of spirit into matter. Singing is an incarnational activity, and it can become a conscious spiritual activity. The Beings at the Threshold do not concern themselves with the earthly definitions or conventions of beauty as might be defined by the classical art world or the commercial recording industry. In Denver, I was brought to my knees by the singers in a little ethno-centric Catholic church in my neighborhood. There were no young people concerned with singing in the choir anymore, so the Italian elderly, and I really mean elderly, sang their way through the Mass each Sunday. I cannot tell you how warbly and bumpy and gnarly their little voices were, singing, stooped over, leaning on their canes, like fragile birds defeathered, necks stretching straight up, defying gravity and common sense. They were not able to hold pitch, nor could they count, but their souls were completely devoted. In this stretching I heard a kind of embodied giving; it redefined humility for me, and I tend to never forget it. The church was filled with light, movement, and currents of fresh sweet air. The love-ray permeated the church. As long as we are still incarnate, as long as we have bodies, we are meant to sing.

> . . . And joying she sings, and singing she longs, but in sweetness
> and heat. . . .
>
> Richard Rolle (1300-1349)

In closing, I would like to introduce you to the works of the Swiss mystic who is named Joa Bolendas.[14] It is to her credit that she has remained virtually unknown. She is alive today, in her late seventies, and is very important to me. She has been receiving angels since she was forty, along with visitations from the Risen Christ, Mary, the four Evangelists, and others. She has lived a contemporary life, with husband and children. She has suffered greatly, spiritually and physically, but meeting her can be compared to meeting a rooted oak tree with a great human heart. She has suffered illness, but she does not resemble the mythos of a frail suffering artist-mystic. Rather, she is a strong, shining transparency, demanding that we storm heaven and pray for the unity of the churches.

The angels sing for her; I have come to call the legacy she has received *visionlieder*. The angels approach her slowly, sometimes over a period of a week. They come to her from afar, gradually coming closer and closer, singing their prayers until she can hold them and give them away to others. She fought this grace; she did not seek it. Over the years, she sacrificed something, she willingly took some things on and gave other things up. In the process, she transformed her direction and meaning, and gradually turned in great responsivity to a higher calling. The world at large does not know this woman; she is not a popular phenomena. She, too, has lived a kind of spiritual silence, in that she has never sought exterior approval

Once, in her home, we were together in the spirit of prayer, and the old monastic proverb came up: "To sing is to pray twice." Though she remembered it warmly, as if greeting an old dear friend, she corrected me like a person on fire. "It is different now. Everything is quickened. . . . Now, to sing is to pray tenfold. . . ."

She instructed me to sing, to sing praise, and to sing with the hands open. I do so, and teach others to do so. I pointed to a painting she had done of one of the angels who comes to her with song. Flames leapt from outstretched angelic hands and a bright light shone in the area where feet would be represented. "Joa," I said, "who is this?" "This is a healing angel. The will must be purified and the hands must be wide open. . . . "

To work with the *visionlieder* of Joa Bolendas, carefully, deeply, repeatedly, and over time, is to work with luminosity and proportion. All of the songs, whether praise or lament, work with light. Light is not meant just to shine, to illuminate, but also to transform. We are meant to sing radiance. When I sang Joa Bolendas' songs for her, she corrected my tempo and told me to move one hand in a slow circular movement, like the angels, like bells. *Sing radiance*; this must be part of the new Jerusalem foretold in the Book of Revelation, foretold by the angels of Budaliget.

Singing is like living *in*, standing *in* someone else's experience. It is about bringing things into existence, and sometimes into balance. When we sing sacred music, it is legitimate to ask, "In whose experience am I standing? Whose story is it? Whose vestments are they?" I think that in cases like Joa Bolendas, the song is the material half of the angel. The actual music is something akin to the breathing of the angels, and allows us to stand, for a moment or an hour, in the experience of the angelic.

Working with the Guardian Angel

Robert Sardello

I want to address the human effort that seems to be required to make connection with the angels. For some, the angels make their appearance in rather startling ways; but how about those of us who have not had such experiences but nonetheless have a real longing for the spiritual worlds? Can some sort of direction be given? Here, a great deal of caution is required because such direction can easily violate the development of individual freedom. What follows is not, therefore, in the manner of a set of instructions but rather the suggestion that meditative practices gradually develop the subtlety of consciousness needed for the apprehension of spiritual beings such as the angels.

We have certain expectations of how an angel ought to appear, and even to act, based upon the kind of consciousness we live in the ordinary world. Do we not expect angels to appear as a kind of alteration of a person we might encounter in the world, maybe more ethereal, or more like a dream image, but in some way perceptible as a distinct being? Perhaps we expect a misty, white clad presence with wings; perhaps a bright light, out of which comes a gentle or a commanding voice; maybe a voice within that is so clear that it is unmistakable that this voice is something other than mere speaking to oneself. Sometimes angels appear in these ways. When, however, it is we who go toward the angels rather than waiting for them to come to us, then it may become necessary to put aside all expectations and set off on a meditative path.

In our enthusiasm for angelic encounters we tend to forget that there are also fallen angels. There are as many tricky and deceptive angelic beings as there are helpful guardians, and one can well imagine that among the bag of tricks of such beings, appearing beneficent and helpful is the best trick of all. It is quite naive to think that all angels are beneficent. How is one to know? This is not an easy question, but the best way is to prepare our own soul life in such a manner that it would at least be possible to test what appears, and this preparation can be best carried out by a meditative practice.

By meditative practice, I here mean a concerted effort, carried out regularly, to intensify the kind of ordinary consciousness we now possess to the point that it becomes possible to have real and accurate impressions of the invisible worlds. The kind of consciousness characteristic of everyday life is the result of a very long process of evolution, something that has been attained over a vast amount of time. The form of meditation that I will draw upon in speaking about working with the guardian angel seeks to approach, gradually, the next phase of the evolution of consciousness. Other forms of meditation go toward the past, toward entering kinds of consciousness that characterized past eons. I am not going to suggest yoga or drumming or chanting, or any form of meditation that dims present awareness; rather, the mode of meditation here suggested involves the intensification of thinking. The background for this form of meditative activity can be found in the work of Rudolf Steiner, particularly his most valuable work, *Knowing Higher Worlds*. I am not standing against other forms of meditation but merely attempting to make clear the tradition I stand within, in which the value of human individual freedom is given the highest respect. The capacity of individual thinking has developed for a purpose; that purpose is not simply to control the outer physical world, but to turn, in freedom, toward the spiritual worlds and eventually to bring about a true spiritual culture.

In ordinary thinking, we are aware of the objects of our thoughts, but not the activity of thinking itself. In meditation that is an intensification of thinking, we think, not about a thing, not even about a non-material thing such as an angel, but within the thing itself. This kind of thinking is not experienced as "head thinking," for it is something that occurs through the whole body. This kind of thinking is like feeling the body as a subtle vessel and you are everywhere within the vessel. Within this vessel there is then brought forth the idea of an angel, a specific angel, say your guardian angel. Then, within this living thought, other thoughts are created in this inner way, thoughts that cohere with the idea of the guardian angel—for example, holding in mind that this angel has been with me for all of my life, that I feel guarded, protected, and guided, but not interfered with. Why is my guardian angel with me? And what is it that makes a guardian angel particular, since an angel is not embodied? As in any meditative practice, intensified thinking must focus and not stray from its activity. The result of such an intensification of thinking can bring love for one's angel; thinking has now entered the realm of the heart.

From a thinking of the heart, it is possible to say more concerning the presence of the guardian angel. The angel is always here, and as always here the angel is difficult to recognize as other than my own consciousness. The first experience of the angel is utter closeness, so it begins to be necessary to attend to this closeness. In meditation, I recognize, on the one hand, my own consciousness. Then, it is as if this ordinary consciousness were surrounded by another presence, almost like myself, but more like myself as I could be rather than as I am. I further realize that my own consciousness can either diverge from this more enveloping presence and do business on its own, so to speak, or I can freely attempt to come closer in balance with the presence that is letting me know constantly a sense of what I could be.

It might be argued that this wider presence, this wider consciousness that seems to include more of me than I am aware of, is mine too, simply the outer edges of myself. But, when there is this relationship of harmony with this presence, I know something that I do not know out of my own separate thoughts—I know who I am destined to become. This knowing, at first, and for a very long time, is in the nature of a clear feeling, not in the form of some bit of information. This sense of destiny is not the same as the information I might receive from the astrologer or the psychic or the diviner. This sense is of a real guiding though completely non-interfering presence, not someone attempting to tell me about myself. The encompassing mantle of this other presence in utter closeness brings a real and tangibly felt sense of my life as a whole. The guardian angel seems to know my life as a whole. Knowing about destiny and feeling within one's destiny are two quite different experiences; in the former, destiny takes the form of something from outside, while in the latter, it is as if our angel carries something for us that we are not quite yet prepared to understand; what the angel carries is far more intimate than any fact of information.

Meditation on the angel has yet another characteristic. The angel is outside us, but is not visible in the way an object or person can be perceived; the angel is there as an intimate, ever so quiet presence. It takes time to approach the angel in a state of complete openness, for we must come close through the heart, through everything we are as a human being. In particular, this means bringing all our dark and ugly qualities, which must be looked upon without judgment, but which are also not concealed. Similarly, we bring all of the qualities of ourselves that are good and true, also looked upon without judgement. These qualities are not enumerated one by one in meditation, but when one meditates on exactly what constitutes openness, it means being as completely human as possible.

Working with the guardian angel brings changes into one's life. It is as if, little by little, what was being carried by our angel begins to be handed over to us; our destiny comes to us when we are able to be responsible for it. The guardian angels protect our destiny, but it is we who retrieve it as we are ready. Everyday life becomes different, often in not particularly enjoyable ways. We begin to see how much of the way we act is influenced by the need to be liked and accepted according to the norms of others, and of our need to look good. As this mask starts to fall away, others may no longer understand us. On the other hand, experiences which were previously categorized as "positive" or "negative" now are felt without these evaluations. Life becomes more interesting, even though outer circumstances may not change very much. We find ourselves on a different path than just getting on with life; we find ourselves on the path of love. No sentimentalism is implied by the word love. No other word is suitable for the attempt to work in accordance with the harmony experienced with the presence of the angel.

The practice of meditation also brings about a new presence of mind, a capacity to see things in a split second that usually go unrecognized. It begins to be possible to catch glimpses of the angel along the edges of our awareness. One morning, for example, I awoke with an inner word resounding loudly and clearly—the word was "activity." I realized in a matter of seconds how passive we tend to be when it comes to spiritual matters. We expect things to come from the angel worlds— messages, instructions, advice, warnings, help. Can we imagine working with the angel as constant activity, the activity of radical receptivity? Being receptive is an extremely active state, and if this activity is not present, spiritual work is filled with spiritual greed, trying to get something from the angel rather than actively getting to know a world that is radically unlike the everyday world of our ordinary consciousness. The aim of getting to know spiritual realities is not simply curiosity, nor is it seeking power. Rather, the aim has to do with becoming more of what we are capable of being and bringing about the possibility of working with the angels to create a world in harmony and balance with the cosmos.

Giving attention to the moment of waking from sleep is one of the most important aspects of developing presence of mind. Waking, the transition from sleep to day consciousness, is the moment our soul and spirit return to the physical body from their nightly sojourn to the soul world and the spirit world. Learning attentiveness to the moment of transition from sleep to waking can be a way of catching real impressions of the soul and spirit worlds. When we are able to be conscious of awaking, there often appear what might be described as objective ideas. By objective idea I mean the presence of idea as a reality more or less independent of my own thought processes. The subjective ideas we have during waking life are like a phantom or a copy of objective ideas, which might better be termed angels. Angel is a better word for what happens than the separate world of ideas in Platonism. For these ideas are living realities, real presences. I recall waking one morning to the presence of a very clear idea, a presence which indicated that nothing in the material world in which we live exists on its own. All that we see around us is the work of the angels. Some of this work was completed long ago; some continues each moment. This came as a true insight, as if this thought was thinking itself through me; I was not thinking in the subjective sense of the word. I did not actually see angels, dream angels, or think about angels. Rather, it was like having, in a second, and in a thought-image rather than a dream picture or sensory image, a complete and full imaginative cognition of the working of the angels. I know now what Jacob Boehme must have felt—on a much smaller scale of course—when he experienced a vision of the creation of the world, a vision which took place in a moment, but which took him twelve years to find the way to speak in his monumental work, *Aurora.*

Learning to work with the angels is to begin living more and more in a different current of time, or to recognize besides the current of time that extends from the past into the present and toward the future, there is an additional current of time that comes from the future into the present. Learning to attend to this time stream, we experience more of what we can be rather than thinking of ourselves in terms of the influences of the past. Angels, I think, "ride" this stream of time, and their concern (particularly guardian angels) is guiding us in our destiny. Our destiny comes to us from the future. There are, of course, all of the effects of the past— heredity, memory, conditioning, talents and abilities—and these too work powerfully in our lives. The angels, however, are primarily concerned with our future, individually as well as with the future of humanity and the future of the world. Working with the angels implies learning to care for what is not yet present, but what is coming to be.

NOTES

ANGELS AND THE SOUL

THOMAS MOORE

1. C. G. Jung, *Collected Works* (Princeton, NJ: Princeton University Press, 1969) 9, 1, par. 268.

2. *St. Bernard's Sermons*, translated by a priest of Mount Melleray (Westminster, MD: The Carroll Press, 1950), 62.

3. *Meister Eckhart: Mystic and Philosopher*, trans. by Reiner Schürmann (Bloomington & London: Indiana University Press, 1978), 9.

4. *Bernard*, 119.

5. Anne C. Emmerich, *The Life of the Blessed Virgin Mary*, trans. by Sir Michael Palairet (Rockford, IL: Tan Books and Publishers, 1954), 142.

6. *Bernard*, 123.

7. Igor Stravinsky, *An Autobiography* (New York: W. W. Norton, 1962), 128.

8. Ficino, *Theologia Platonica, Omnia Opera* (1559), p.79, 119; and Paul O. Kristeller, *The Philosophy of Marcelio Ficino*, trans. by Virginia Conant (Gloucester, MA: Peter Smith, 1964), 106.

ROBERT D. ROMANYSHYN

1. The passage is the opening of the second elegy in Rainer Maria Rilke, *Duino Elegies*, trans. J. B. Leishman and Stephen Spender (New York: W. W. Norton, 1939), 29. I must acknowledge my debt and gratitude to Eva Spork whose doctoral work on Rilke has deepened my appreciation of the Angel.

2. Rilke, Ibid., 69–71.

3. Ibid., 21.

4. See Tom Moore's presentation in this volume.

5. The hegemony of vision, the rule of "the despotic eye," is developed in Robert Romanyshyn, "The Despotic Eye," *The Changing Reality of Modern Man, Essays in honor of J. H. van den Berg*, ed. Dreyer Kruger (Capetown: Juta and Co., 1984).

6. It is not possible to do more than offer this brief summary of linear perspective vision. The full story of its origins and development as the

cultural–historical psychology of modern scientific–technological consciousness is told in Robert Romanyshyn, *Technology as Symptom & Dream* (New York and London: Routledge, 1989).

GAIL THOMAS

1. I am indebted to William Bloom's insightful monograph, *Devas, Fairies, and Angels: A Modern Approach* (Glastonbury: Gothic Image, 1986).

2. The opening words to "The First Elegy" of R. M. Rilke's *Duino Elegies*, trans. Stephen Garmey and Jay Wilson (New York: Harper & Row, 1972).

3. Joscelyn Godwin, *Robert Fludd: Hermetic Philosopher and Surveyor of Two Worlds* (Boston: Shambhala Publications, 1979).

4. Gustav Davidson, *A Dictionary of Angels* (New York: Free Press, 1967), 240.

5. Rudolf Steiner, *The Four Seasons and the Archangels* (New York: Rudolf Steiner Press, 1984), 54, 57.

PACO MITCHELL

1. C. G. Jung, *Collected Works* (Princeton, N.J.: Princeton University Press, 1971), 6, Paragraph 174.

ANGELS AND SCIENCE

LARRY DOSSEY

1. Martin Lings, *Studies in Comparative Religion* vol. 4, no. 1 (Winter 1970): 59, quoted in Huston Smith, *Beyond the Post–Modern Mind* (Wheaton: Theosophical Publishing House, 1982), 174.

2. Marshall Sahlins, *Culture and Practical Reason* (Chicago: University of Chicago Press, 1976), 52–53.

3. Andrew P. Smith, "Mutiny on *The Beagle*," *ReVision*, Vol. 7, No. 1, Spring 1984.

4. Arthur Koestler, *Janus: A Summing Up* (New York: Random House, 1978).

5. Huston Smith, *Beyond the Post–Modern Mind* (Wheaton: Theosophical Publishing House, 1982).

6. Jacques Monod, *Chance and Necessity* (New York: Random House, 1972), 21.

7. C. H. Waddington, *The Strategy of the Genes* (London: Allen and Unwin, 1957), 64–5.

8. Smith, 170.

9. Koestler, 166.

10. Pierre Grassé, *Evolution of Living Organisms: Evidence for a New Theory of Transformation* (New York: Academic Press, 1977), 104.

11. Smith, 173.

12. See Steven Stanley, "Darwin Done Over," *The Sciences* (October 1981): 19.

13. Arthur Lovejoy, *The Great Chain of Being* (Cambridge: Harvard University Press, 1936), 56, 26.

14. Smith, 40.

15. Aldous Huxley, *The Perennial Philosophy* (New York: Harper & Brothers, 1945).

16. Ken Wilber, *Up From Eden* (New York: Doubleday, 1981), 295 ff.

17. Wilber, 301.

18. Werner Heisenberg, *Physics and Beyond* (New York: Harper & Row, 1971), 114.

19. Niels Bohr, quoted in Heisenberg, 114.

20. See Sir John Eccles and Daniel N. Robinson, "Self–Consciousness and the Human Person," *The Wonder of Being Human* (Boston: New Science Library, 1985), 25–45.

21. Nicolas Berdyaev, *The Destiny of Man* (New York: Harper and Row, 1960).

22. Wilber, 298.

23. Berdyaev, quoted in Wilber, 317.

24. John Cairns, "The Origin of Mutants," *Nature*, vol. 355, no. 6186: 142–145.

25. Susumu Ohno and Midori Ohno, "The All Pervasive Principle of Repetitious Recurrence Governs Not Only Coding Sequence Construction But Also Human Endeavor in Musical Composition," *Immuno-genetics* 24 (1986): 71–78; Susumu Ohno and Marty Jabara, "Repeats of Base Oligomers (N = 3n + 1 or 2) as Immortal Coding Sequences of the Primeval World: Construction of Coding Sequences is Based Upon the Principle of Musical Composition," *Chemica Scripta* 26B (1986): 43–49.

FREDERICK TURNER

1. R. M. Rilke, Duino Elegies, trans. J. B. Leishman and Stephen Spender (London: Hogarth Press, 1963), 33.

ANGELS AND IMAGINATION

LOUISE COWAN

1. The quotations from the *Divine Comedy* are taken from the translation by Charles S. Singleton (Princeton: Bollingen Series, Princeton Univ. Press, 1980).

2. John Milton, *Paradise Lost*, ed. Scott Elledge (New York & London: Norton Critical Edition, W. W. Norton , 1975).

DONA S. GOWER

1. Quoted in Allan Tate, *Collected Essays* (Denver: Alan Swallow, 1959), 445.

2. Ibid., 453.

3. Ibid., 454.

4. John Milton, *Paradise Lost*, ed. Scott Elledge (New York & London: Norton Critical Edition, W. W. Norton, 1975).

5. Georg Lukacs, *The Theory of the Novel*, trans. Anna Bostock (London: Merlin Press, 1978), 56.

6. Ibid., 97.

7. Ibid., 118.

8. Richard Wilbur, *The Poems of Richard Wilbur* (New York: Harcourt, Brace & World, 1963), 65.

ROBERT TRAMMELL

1. Charles Olson, "Maximus, at the Harbor," *Maximus Poems IV, V, VI* (London: Cape Goliard Press, 1968).

2. J. B. Beer, *Coleridge the Visionary* (New York: Collier Books, 1962), 78.

3. L. A. G. Strong, "Reminiscences of W. B. Yeats," *The Listener*, April 22, 1954; cited by
J. B. Beer in *Coleridge the Visionary*, no page number given.

4. Beer, 78.

5. *The Vimalakirti Nirdesa Sutra*, trans. Charles Luk (Berkeley and London: Shambhala, 1972), 140.

6. See William Gray, *The Ladder of Lights (or Quabalah Renovata)* (Gloucester, England: Helios Books, 1968).

7. Pat Berry, "Stopping: A Mode of Animation," *Echo's Subtle Body* (Dallas: Spring Publications, 1982), 160.

8. See Karl Kerényi, *Athene* (Dallas: Spring Publications, 1988).

9. Gray, 127.

10. C. G. Jung, *Collected Works* (Princeton, N.J.: Princeton University Press, 1967) 13, par. 108.

11. Papus, *The Tarot of the Bohemians,* trans. A. P. Morton (New York: Arcanum Books, 1958), 164.

12. Titus Burckhardt, *Alchemy* (Baltimore: Penguin Books, 1974), 131.

13. *Collected Works* 12, par. 404.

14. *Collected Works* 13, par. 118.

15. Burckhardt, 131

16. D. H. Lawrence, *The Plumed Serpent* (New York: Vintage Books, 1959).

17. *The Dhammapada,* trans. Juan Mascaró (Baltimore: Penguin Books, 1973), 38.

JOANNE STROUD

1. Gaston Bachelard, *The Right to Dream,* trans. J. A. Underwood (Dallas: The Dallas Institute Publications, 1989), 96.

2. Gaston Bachelard, *Air and Dreams: An Essay On the Imagination of Movement,* trans. Edith R. and C. Frederick Farrell (Dallas: The Dallas Institute Publications, 1988), 10-11.

3. *The Right to Dream,* 97.

4. *Air and Dreams,* 59.

5. Ibid., 60.

6. Ibid., 58.

7. Ibid., 54ff, 75.

8. *The Right to Dream,* 95.

9. Emanuel Swedenborg, *Heaven and Hell* (New York: Swedenborg Foundation Inc., 1984), 69.

10. Ibid., 71.

11. *The Right to Dream,* 96.

12. Ibid., 96.

13. *Heaven and Hell,* 72.

14. Ibid., 207.

15. *Air and Dreams,* 58.

16. *The Right to Dream,* 97.

17. Ibid., 94.

18. Ibid., 94.

19. Ibid., 93.

20. *Air and Dreams,* 40.

21. *The Right to Dream,* 98.

EILEEN GREGORY

1. William Loftus Hare, *Mysticism of East and West* (London: J. Cape, 1923), 307. For directing me to this quotation I am indebted to the discussion of H.D.'s *Trilogy* in Susan Friedman, *Psyche Reborn: The Emergence of H.D.* (Bloomington: Indiana University Press, 1982), 218.

2. Quotations in this paper from *The Walls Do Not Fall* and *Tribute to the Angels* will refer to the edition *Trilogy* (New York: New Directions, 1973). References will be given in the text in abbreviated form (*The Walls Do Not Fall* as WDNF and *Tribute to the Angels* as TA); numbers will refer to sections of the cited poem.

3. For a discussion of the Kabbalistic concept of the breaking-of-the-vessels, originating with the sixteenth century writer Isaac Luria, see Harold Bloom, *Kabbalah and Criticism* (New York: Seabury Press, 1975), 38-43.

4. For a discussion of the hieroglyphs of "Luxor bee, chick, and hare," see Rosie King-Smyth, "The Spell of the Luxor Bee," *San José Studies* 13.3 (Fall 1987): 78-79.

5. Bloom, 100.

6. See James Hillman, "Silver and the White Earth (Part One)," *Spring* (1980): 24.

7. s.v. "Uriel" in Gustav Davidson, *A Dictionary of Angels* (New York: The Free Press, 1967).

8. My discussion of bitterness and salt is indebted to James Hillman, "Salt: A Chapter in Alchemical Psychology," *Images of the Untouched: Virginity in Psyche, Myth and Community*, ed. Joanne Stroud and Gail Thomas (Dallas: Spring Publications), 111-37.

9. s.v. "Annael" in *A Dictionary of Angels*.

10. On green as a stage following *nigredo*, see C.G. Jung, *Psychology and Alchemy*, 2nd ed., trans. R.F.C. Hull (Princeton: Princeton University Press, 1968), 229. On blue as a transitional stage between black and white, see James Hillman, "Alchemical Blue and the *Unio Mentalis*," *Sulphur* 1 (1981): 33-50.

ANGELS AND ART

LYLE NOVINSKI

Drawings by Lyle Novinski from the work of the following artists:
1. Detail, *Theodora and Retinue*, San Vitale, Ravenna, 526-47.
2. Angel from Pala D'Oro, San Marco, Venice.

3. Angel detail, *Coronation of the Virgin*, Pinturicchio, 1459.

4. Angel, Giotto, *Crucifixion*, Arena Chapel, Padua, 1306.

5. *Annunciation*, Jan Van Eyck, 1428.

6. *Concert of the Angels*, detail, Isenheim Altarpiece, Matthias Gruenewald, 1515.

7. *Angel*, Melozzo da Forli, 1478.

8. Detail, Ceiling Fresco of San Ignazio, Andrea Pozzo, 1691-94.

Mary Vernon

1. A. B. Davidson, "Angels," Hastings' *Dictionary of the Bible*, I:95 as quoted by Arnold Whittick, *Symbols: Signs and their Meaning and Uses in Design* (Newton, Massachusetts: Charles T. Branford, 1971), 197.

Practical Work with the Angels

Therese Shroeder-Sheker

1. Part of this material was originally presented by the author at a *Mystics Quarterly* session at the 26th International Congress on Medieval Studies at the Medieval Institute (Western Michigan University) in Kalamazoo, Michigan in 1991. The contents of that paper and this presentation are excerpted from a much larger work of the same title, to be published by St. Dunstan's Press in early 1995. The fully developed work explores the multiple levels of the mystical experience of the "loss of freedom," and compares the diaries, visions and poetry, and medical records of medieval and contemporary people as patients and prisoners.

2. See Denise Restout and Robert Hawkins, *Landowska on Music*, (Briarcliff Manor, NY: Stein and Day, 1969).

3. Gitta Mallasz, *Talking with Angels*, (Einsiedeln, Switzerland: Daimon Verlag, 1988.

4. See the *Cauda Pavonis: Hermetic Text Society Newsletter*, vol.5, no.2, published by Washington State University at Pullman.

5. See Otto von Simpson, *The Gothic Cathedral: Origins of Gothic Architecture and the Medieval Concept of Order*, especially the entire second chapter entitled "Measure and Light," (Princeton: Bollingen Series, Princeton Univ. Press, 1984).

6. At the time of this revision, June 1994, I have been notified that Gitta has recently passed away.

7. See Abram Tertz (Andrei Sinyavski), *A Voice from the Chorus*, translated by Kyril Fitzlyon and Max Hayward for Farrar, Straus and Giroux, 1957. Also, volumes one and two of Aleksandr Solzhenitsyn's *Gulag Archipelago*, Avraham Shifrin's *Fourth Dimension*, and Phanine's *Experiences in Sologdin*.

8. See Anders Nyberg, *Freedom is Coming: Songs of Protest and Praise from South Africa*, published by the Church of Sweden Mission in Uppsala, Sweden.

9. See Rabbi Halevy Donin, *To Pray As a Jew*, (New York: Harper Collins, 1980).

10. See Daniel Chanan Matt's translation for Paulist Press Classics of Western Spirituality, *Zohar: The Book of Enlightenment (1982)*. See also Joscelyn Godwin, *Harmonies of Heaven and Earth: the Spiritual Dimensions of Music*, (Rochester, VT: Inner Traditions, 1987).

11. See *Aretha Franklin: 30 Greatest Hits*, on Atlantic 81668-2. Also *Aretha: Gospel*, on Chess CH-C-91521.

12. See John Gorka, *Land of the Bottom Line*, on High Street-Windham Hill WD 1089.

13. Rudolf Steiner says something very similar in the classic *Knowledge of the Higher Worlds*: "Every idea which does not become your ideal slays a force in your soul; every idea which becomes your ideal creates within you life-forces." See Christopher Bamford's superlative new translation, *How to Know Higher Worlds* (New York: Anthroposophic Press, 1994).

14. See a forthcoming critical edition of the Joa Bolendas material to be published by Lindisfarne Press.

SELECT BIBLIOGRAPHY

Adler, Mortimer J. *The Angels and Us*. New York: Macmillan, 1988.

Bachelard, Gaston. *Air and Dreams: An Essay On the Imagination of Movement*. Trans. Edith R. and C. Frederick Farrell. Dallas: Dallas Institute Publications, 1988.

————. *The Right to Dream*. Trans. J. A. Underwood. Dallas: Dallas Institute Publications, 1989.

Beer, J. B. *Coleridge the Visionary*. New York: Collier Books, 1962.

Berdyaev, Nicolas. *The Destiny of Man*. New York: Harper and Row, 1960.

Bernard of Clairvaux. *St. Bernard's Sermons*. Trans. A Priest of Mount Melleray. Westminster, MD: Carroll Press, 1950.

Berry, Patricia. "Stopping: A Mode of Animation." *Echo's Subtle Body*. Dallas: Spring   Publications, 1982.

Bloom, Harold. *Kabbalah and Criticism*. New York: Seabury Press, 1975.

Bloom, William. *Devas, Fairies, and Angels: A Modern Approach*. Glastonbury: Gothic Image, 1986.

Boros, Ladislaus. *Angels and Men*. UK: Search Press, 1990.

Burckhardt, Titus. *Alchemy*. Baltimore: Penguin Books, 1974.

Cairns, John. "The Origin of Mutants." *Nature*, vol. 355, no. 6186: 142–145.

Cowan, Donald. "Science, History, and the Evidence of Things Not Seen." In *From Parnassus: Essays in Honor of Jacques Barzun*. Ed. Weiner, Dora B., and William R. Keylor. New York: Harper & Row, 1976.

Daniélou, Jean. *The Angels and Their Mission*. Westminster, MD: Christian Classics, 1987.

Dante Alighieri. *The Divine Comedy*. Translated by Charles S. Singleton. Princeton: Bollingen Series, Princeton Univ. Press, 1980.

Davidson, Gustav. *A Dictionary of Angels*. New York: Free Press, 1967.

Donin, Rabbi Halevy. *To Pray As a Jew*. New York: Harper Collins, 1980.

H.D. (Hilda Doolittle). *Trilogy*. New York: New Directions, 1973.

Eccles, Sir John, and Daniel N. Robinson. "Self–Consciousness and the Human Person." *The Wonder of Being Human*. Boston: New Science Library, 1985.

Emmerich, Anne C. *The Life of the Blessed Virgin Mary*. Trans. by Sir Michael Palairet. Rockford: Tan Books and Publishers, 1954.

Friedman, Susan. *Psyche Reborn: The Emergence of H.D.* Bloomington: Indiana University Press, 1982.

Godwin, Joscelyn. *Harmonies of Heaven and Earth: the Spiritual Dimensions of Music*. Rochester, VT: Inner Traditions, 1987.

———. *Robert Fludd: Hermetic Philosopher and Surveyor of Two Worlds*. Boston: Shambhala Publications, 1979.

Grassé, Pierre. *Evolution of Living Organisms: Evidence for a New Theory of Transformation*. New York: Academic Press, 1977.

Gray, William. *The Ladder of Lights (or Quabalah Renovata)*. Gloucester, England: Helios Books, 1968.

Hare, William Loftus. *Mysticism of East and West*. London: J. Cape, 1923.

Heisenberg, Werner. *Physics and Beyond*. New York: Harper & Row, 1971.

Hillman, James. "Alchemical Blue and the *Unio Mentalis*." *Sulphur* 1 (1981).

———. "Salt: A Chapter in Alchemical Psychology." *Images of the Untouched: Virginity in Psyche, Myth and Community*. Ed. Joanne Stroud and Gail Thomas. Dallas: Spring Publications, 1982.

———. "Silver and the White Earth (Part One)." *Spring: A Journal of Archetype and Culture* (1980).

Huxley, Aldous. *The Perennial Philosophy*. New York: Harper & Brothers, 1945.

Jung, C. G. *Collected Works*. Princeton, NJ: Princeton University Press, 1969.

———. *Psychology and Alchemy*. 2nd ed. Trans. R.F.C. Hull. Princeton: Princeton University Press, 1968.

Kerényi, Karl. *Athene*. Dallas: Spring Publications, 1988.

King-Smyth, Rosie. "The Spell of the Luxor Bee." *San José Studies* 13.3 (Fall 1987).

Koestler, Arthur. *Janus: A Summing Up*. New York: Random House, 1978.

Lawrence, D. H. *The Plumed Serpent*. New York: Vintage Books, 1959.

Lovejoy, Arthur. *The Great Chain of Being*. Cambridge: Harvard University Press, 1936.

Luk, Charles, trans. *The Vimalakirti Nirdesa Sutra*. Berkeley & London: Shambhala, 1972.

Lukacs, Georg. *The Theory of the Novel*. Trans. Anna Bostock. London: Merlin Press, 1978.

Maclean, Dorothy. *To Hear the Angels Sing: An Odyssey of Co-Creation with the Devic Kingdom*. Hudson: Lindisfarne Press, 1990.

Mallasz, Gitta. *Talking with Angels*. Einsiedeln, Swietzerland: Daimon Verlag, 1988.

Mascaró, Juan, trans. *The Dhammapada*. Baltimore: Penguin Books, 1973.

Matt, Daniel C., trans. *Zohar: The Book of Enlightenment*. Mahwah, NJ: Classics of Western Spirituality Series, Paulist Press, 1982.

Milton, John. *Paradise Lost*. Ed. Scott Elledge. New York & London: Norton Critical Edition, W. W. Norton, 1975.

Monod, Jacques. *Chance and Necessity*. New York: Random House, 1972.

Moolenburgh, H. C. *A Handbook of Angels*. Woodstock: Beekman, 1994.

Nyberg, Anders. *Freedom is Coming: Songs of Protest and Praise from South Africa*. Uppsala, Sweden: The Church of Sweden Mission, n.d.

Ohno, Susumu, and Midori Ohno. "The All Pervasive Principle of Repetitious Recurrence Governs Not Only Coding Sequence Construction But Also Human Endeavor in Musical Composition." *Immuno-genetics* 24 (1986).

Ohno, Susumu, and Marty Jabara. "Repeats of Base Oligomers (N = 3n + 1 or 2) as Immortal Coding Sequences of the Primeval World: Construction of Coding Sequences is Based Upon the Principle of Musical Composition." *Chemica Scripta* 26B (1986).

Olson, Charles. "Maximus, at the Harbor." *Maximus Poems IV, V, VI* . London: Cape Goliard Press, 1968.

Papus, *The Tarot of the Bohemians*. Trans. A. P. Morton. New York: Arcanum Books, 1958.

Restout, Denise and Robert Hawkins. *Landowska on Music*. Briarcliff Manor, NY: Stein and Day, 1969.

Rilke, R. M. *Duino Elegies*. Trans. Stephen Garmey and Jay Wilson. New York: Harper & Row, 1972.

Romanyshyn, Robert. *Technology as Symptom & Dream*. New York and London: Routledge, 1989.

———. "The Despotic Eye." *The Changing Reality of Modern Man, Essays in honor of J. H. van den Berg*. Ed. Dreyer Kruger. Capetown: Juta and Co., 1984.

Sahlins, Marshall. *Culture and Practical Reason*. Chicago: University of Chicago Press, 1976.

Schürmann, Reiner, trans. *Meister Eckhart: Mystic and Philosopher*. Bloomington & London: Indiana University Press, 1978.

Smith, Andrew P. "Mutiny on *The Beagle*." *ReVision*, Vol. 7, No. 1 (Spring 1984).

Smith, Huston. *Beyond the Post–Modern Mind*. Wheaton: Theosophical Publishing House, 1982.

Stanley, Steven. "Darwin Done Over." *The Sciences* (October 1981).

Steiner, Rudolf. *The Four Seasons and the Archangels*. New York: Rudolf Steiner Press, l984.

———. *Genesis: Secrets of the Bible Story of Creation*. Trans. Dorothy Lenn, et al. New York: Anthroposophic Press, 1982.

———. *How to Know Higher Worlds: A Modern Path of Initiation*. Trans. Christopher Bamford. Hudson, NY: Anthroposophic Press, 1994.

———. *Knowledge of the Higher Worlds and its Attainment*. Hudson, NY: Anthroposophic Press, 1947.

———. *What Does the Angel Do in Our Astral Body*. Mokelumne Hill, Ca: Mokelumne Hill Press, 1960.

Stravinsky, Igor. *An Autobiography*. New York: W. W. Norton, 1962.

Strong, L. A. G. "Reminiscences of W. B. Yeats." *The Listener* (April 22, 1954).

Swedenborg, Emanuel. *Heaven and Hell*. New York: Swedenborg Fndn., 1984.

Tate, Allan. *Collected Essays*. Denver: Alan Swallow, 1959.

Tertz, Abram (Andrei Sinyavski). *A Voice from the Chorus*. Trans. Kyril   Fitzlyon and Max Hayward. New York: Farrar, Straus and Giroux, 1957.

von Simpson, Otto. *The Gothic Cathedral: Origins of Gothic Architecture and the Medieval Concept of Order*. Princeton: Bollingen Series, Princeton Univ. Press,1984.

Waddington, C. H. *The Strategy of the Genes*. London: Allen and Unwin, 1957.

Whittick, Arnold. *Symbols: Signs and their Meaning and Uses in Design*. Newton, MA: Charles T. Branford, 1971.

Wilber, Ken. *Up From Eden*. New York: Doubleday, 1981.

Wilbur, Richard. *The Poems of Richard Wilbur*. New York: Harcourt, Brace & World, 1963.

Contributors

DONALD COWAN, PH.D., Physicist; University Professor,
University of Dallas

LOUISE COWAN, PH.D., Literary critic; University Professor,
University of Dallas

LARRY DOSSEY, M.D., Scholar of medicine and healing

DONA S. GOWER, PH.D., Director of the Dallas Institute's
Teachers Academy

EILEEN GREGORY, PH.D., Chairman, Department of English, The
University of Dallas

PACO MITCHELL, PH.D., Practicing Analyst in Port Townsend,
Washington

THOMAS MOORE, PH.D., Author; Founder, Institute for the
Study of Imagination

LYLE NOVINSKI, Artist; Chairman of the Art Department of the
University of Dallas

ROBERT D. ROMANYSHYN, Practicing Psychologist; Faculty,
Pacifica Institute

ROBERT SARDELLO, PH.D., Co-Founder of the School of
Spiritual Psychology

THERESE SCHROEDER-SHEKER, Founder-Director, Chalice of Repose Project, St. Patrick's Hospital of Missoula, Montana

CYNTHIA SMITH STIBOLT, Artist, Santa Fe, New Mexico

JOANNE STROUD, PH.D., Author; Director of The Dallas Institute Publications

GAIL THOMAS, PH.D., Cultural Critic; Director of the Dallas Institute

ROBERT TRAMMELL, Poet

FREDERICK TURNER, PH.D., Poet, Founders Professor of Arts and Humanities, The University of Texas at Dallas

MARY VERNON, Artist; Chair, Studio Arts Division, Meadows Schoolof the Arts, Southern Methodist University

Acknowledgments

The editor and publisher gratefully acknowledge permission from the following sources to reprint material in this book:

"Love Calls Us to the Things of This World" from *Things of This World*, copyright © 1956 and renewed 1984 by Richard Wilbur, reprinted by permission of Harcourt Brace & Company.

Excerpts from *The Duino Elegies* by Rainer Maria Rilke, translated by Stephen Garmey and Harold J. Wilson. Copyright © 1972 by Stephen Garmey and Jay Wilson. Introduction copyright © 1972 by Stephen Garmey. Reprinted by permission of HarperCollins Publishers, Inc.

H.D.: Collected Poems 1912–1944. Copyright © 1982 by The Estate of Hilda Doolittle. Reprinted by permission of New Directions Publishing Corp.

Reprinted from *Duino Elegies* by Rainer Maria Rilke, translated from the German by J. B. Leishman and Stephen Spender, with the permission of W. W. Norton & Company, Inc. Copyright 1939 by W. W. Norton & Company, Inc., renewed © 1967 by Stephen Spender and J. B. Leishman.